PREACHING WHILE BLEEDING

Is There A Prophet in the House?

H. BEECHER HICKS, JR.

Urban Ministries, Inc.

FIRST UMI EDITION

Copyright © 2018 by H. Beecher Hicks, Jr.
hbeecherhicksministries.com
All rights reserved.

No part of this book may be reproduced or transmitted in any form or by any means, electronic or mechanical, including photocopying, recording, video, or by any information or retrieval system, without prior written permission from the publisher except for the use of brief quotations in a book review.

Published in the United States by Urban Ministries, Inc.
P. O. Box 436987
Chicago, IL 60643
www. urbanministries. com 1-800-860-8642

ISBN 978-1-68353-000-8 (paperback)
ISBN 978-1-68353-001-5 (ebook)

LIBRARY OF CONGRESS CONTROL NUMBER: 2017952804

Cover design by Laura Duffy
Book design by Astrid Lewis Reedy

Printed in the United States of America

TO
Elizabeth
After fifty-three years
still my bride

AND TO MY CHILDREN
H. Beecher, III
Ivan Douglas
Kristin Elizabeth
Crystal
Christia

AND TO OUR GRANDCHILDREN—
OUR JOY, OUR FUTURE AND OUR HOPE
Austynn Lene
Ashley Rene
H. Beecher, IV
Harrison Patton
Anya Madison

Contents

AFRICAN-AMERICAN PREACHING:
BY DEFINITION / 9

PREFACE / 11

FOREWORDS / 15
I. Bishop John R Bryant
II. Bishop J. Douglas Wiley Taylor

......

INTRODUCTION
Thoughts on Preaching / 21

Thoughts on Bleeding and the Blood / 28
- The Authority of Scripture
- Theology before Methodology
- Three Seminarians: Meaning, Relevance, and Will It Preach?

. 1 .
Preaching Matters / 52

. 2 .
The Process of Preaching / 65
"How Shall They Preach?"

. 3 .
The Prophetic Pulpit — Part I / 97
To Prophesy or Not?

. 4 .
The Prophetic Pulpit — Part II / *125*
Proclamation in Perilous Times: The Elijah Paradigm

. 5 .
The Prophetic Pulpit — Part III / *157*
Preaching While Bleeding

. 6 .
A Passion for Preaching / *202*

. 7 .
A Question for Preachers / *217*
"Are You Serious?"

. 8 .
A Closing Word / *248*
"And So I Preached Jesus"

......

APPENDIX / *272*

BIBLIOGRAPHY / *277*

ABOUT THE AUTHOR / *281*

READING GROUP GUIDE / *283*

...

African-American Preaching: By Definition

Broadly defined, all preaching is the out-breathing of the Word of God through the agency of the Holy Spirit, incarnate in Jesus Christ.

Our preaching, however, has been entrusted to feeble hands and lisping tongues.

... More than mere oratory; it is the continuing and unceasing movement on the part of the Eternal to make protestations of God's love for God's people.

... More than words on a page, more than the parade of spiritual phrases designed to attract the wandering attentions of mankind, our preaching is God's way of using human hearts, no matter the culture, no matter the gender, and filling those mouths with God's Word.

African American preaching, however, is born of a different dimension. African American preaching is the gift of God to those who have been sent to speak to and for the oppressed and the downtrodden; it is a kind of Holy, anointed articulation designed to "rescue the perishing and care for the dying."

This preaching encourages prophets among us to preach from and to a cultural context that sees rhetoric as a path to action and finds its power to prevail in the redemptive and salvific blood of our Christ. It is that preaching that is stirred in a cauldron of pain; it is proclamation emanating from deep within a poisoned pot. Strangely, whether this preaching starts with pain or poison, authentic African American preaching finds its way to "unspeakable joy!"

It is the witness of those who have felt the brush of angels' wings on trembling lips at the altar; it is the testimony of a tongue that has been set on fire, and is yet available to those who would step aside from the fiery furnace. Our preaching must always be relevant to one's social condition and always available to speak truth to power. It is the only Word that can lift us from the "Underground" to "Higher Ground." Upon this ground the whole of this writing stands.

H. BEECHER HICKS, JR.
Mitchellville, Maryland
September 2017

Preface

The writing of this text is neither happenstance nor a twist of fate, whatever that imposter may be. I assure you my writing through this learning tool is neither contrived nor artificial in any way. Now in the third year of my retirement from an active, congregation-based ministry, I find myself being closed in by the walls of my home, in search of a Word from the Lord, or at least an answer to the question: What now? The answers have been eclectic.

One such answer to my question came in the form of a conversation with one of my "Sons in the Ministry," Dr. Leonard N. Smith, Pastor of the Mt. Zion Baptist Church of Alexandria, Virginia. Dr. Smith is a gifted preacher, a biblical scholar, theologically alert, an administrative genius, and a brother beloved.

We were on our way to lunch, as I recall it, and Leonard was filled with ideas of what I should do with the rest of my life. I paid attention. It seemed as though I did have a need to expose or to offer whatever gift I have remaining to the swift stroke of my pen but most especially to the will of God for my life. Leonard would not leave well enough alone and added a codicil to his suggestions.

"Hicks, I know what your next move should be. First of all," he expressed with restrained enthusiasm, "I need you to attend a conference in Orlando, Florida of the Global United Fellowship, under the anointed leadership of Bishop Neal C. Ellis. They have a Pastor's Conference that is a part of the larger Fellowship. We would like for you to become a part of us, bring a lecture on the theme, and take the reins of leadership for approximately 1,000 pastors." And he went on, "This will be a fitting addendum to the long years of your ministry. This new generation of preachers needs to hear what you have to say! You will really be a gift to the body of Christ."

He wasn't through. "Brother Pastor," as he calls me, "I even know the title of your next book. This is it: PREACHING WHILE BLEEDING. I had to admit I was intrigued with the thought. It's the kind of thought that makes one want to say, "Hmm!"

I put the whole discussion on the table and put this writing work he was suggesting on "hold." After I made sure he paid for lunch, (Age really does have its privileges!) I went on my way. I would hear about this more quickly than I knew.

Months later, I went off to preach in the state of my birth, Louisiana. As is often the case in New Orleans, the humidity was out of control and thermostats were of no use. There's no other way to say it, it was hot! At the wheel was my dear friend, Bishop J. D. Wiley-Taylor, Presiding Prelate of the Life Center Cathedral in New Orleans. Our conversation was free ranging and, as I feared, the discussion would go toward me and my future. Soon thereafter, I told J. D. of my conversation with Leonard Smith. As I described the work to Bishop Wiley, his response was visceral. His response to the notion of a book on bleeding while preaching was both reasoned and biblically instructive. The die was cast.

I was convinced that this was not the word of Leonard Smith or J. D. Wiley. Something else was being communicated from a Source I had heard from before. God's voice speaking, His will was inescapable and undeniable. Thus began the preparatory work necessary for the production of the volume you now hold in your hands.

There are several persons to whom I owe a deep debt of gratitude: Bishop Leonard Smith and Bishop J. D. Wiley for claiming me as brother and sharing with me their wise counsel. The Reverend Faith Bynoe, for her invaluable scholarly, intuitive, and critical feedback provided for the initial editing of the desktop draft.

Special thanks to Ms. Constance McCrimmon, Rev. Edith Daniels and Reverend Adriane Blair Wise who worked hard keeping my schedule, keeping appointments running on time and my office in some order. Thanks to Reverend Granville Seward who always had a listening ear when I needed to run a paragraph by his insightful and critical point of view.

I am especially thankful for the willingness of Dr. Jeffrey Wright, CEO of Urban Ministries, Inc. for making this publication happen. Moreover, I am grateful to Dr. Jeffrey Haggray, Executive Minister of the Home Missions Board of the American Baptist Churches, Dr. Edward Harding, Senior Minister, Prince Georges Presbyterian Church, and of course, Dr. Leonard N. Smith, Senior Minister of the Mt. Zion Church in Arlington, Virginia, each for their wise counsel and needed criticism of this volume.

No words can be gathered to sufficiently express my love for my wife, Elizabeth Jean, who has put up with my far-reaching preaching assignments and for my daughter, Kristin, who will always be my precious baby girl. Finally, I acknowledge my children and their spouses, H. Beecher III (Crystal), Ivan Douglas (Christia), and Kristin Elizabeth, as well as my grandchildren, Austynn Lene, Ashley Rene, Anya Madison, H. Beecher IV, and Harrison Patton. They are, collectively, the "apple of my eye." I love them all!!

Fifty years in the pastoral ministry is a long run; but for me it has been a good run. Through 37 of those years, Metropolitan has been a faithful, patient, and prayerful people.

Remember: He will build His Church "and the gates of hell shall not prevail against it!"

. . .

Foreword I

I have known H. Beecher Hicks, Jr., for forty-five years. I have known him as a scholarly student, as a loving family man, as a gifted singer, as a powerful preacher, and as a prolific writer. Dr. H. Beecher's gifts have been a blessing to many; but I believe that it is his writing gift that has taken him further into the lives and circumstances of congregations, pastors, and clergy families. This, his latest offering, will be no exception.

Preaching While Bleeding is a volume that deals not only with the "art and science" of sermon preparation and delivery. It is a gift that Dr. Hicks has taught at the seminary level and practiced the art of preaching now for more than fifty years. Not only is he able to teach the reader what to do—in this volume he does an excellent job in that regard—but there is no one who does a better job of modeling the preaching moment.

Don't put this book down until you have fully read his sermon in chapter seven. As good and as necessary as it is for the preacher to know and practice the "art and science" of sermon preparation and delivery, what makes this volume so important is that our writer spends quality time addressing the discipline and demands that are made on the one who preaches. Our author makes the case by using the metaphor, "bleeding," in order to drive home how demanding the life of an authentic proclaimer is.

The demands of ministry are so weighty they require your life's blood, your very soul. The preacher must submit to the will of God. To do that, H. Beecher Hicks believes you must enter in a personal relationship with God to know God. This relationship requires that the preacher be a practitioner of the spiritual disciplines: a strong prayer life, time must be spent with the Holy Scriptures, and quiet time for the purpose of meditation.

None of this causes the preacher to "bleed." The bleeding comes when the God who calls sends the preacher into the world. The preacher is sent to the poor, the oppressed, the marginalized, the misguided, the weak, the confused, the spiritually lost, and to those who hurt. This is when the bleeding begins. Dr. Hicks writes that the preacher is sent to deliver a Prophetic Word, a word of liberation, forgiveness, and empowerment. And this assignment must often be carried out while bleeding.

H. Beecher Hicks, Jr., eloquently writes that help is available to those who preach from sources that must be nurtured. Help comes from the God who calls, from the Gospel that is preached, and from your family. These sources must be protected and appreciated. Fundamentally, the greatest resource of the preacher is the faith that you preach to others.

As one who also bleeds, I can say with complete certainty that this volume will become a necessary help to be read and re-read, to be quoted, and to be recommended to others. You will be both inspired and empowered.

BISHOP JOHN R BRYANT
Presiding Bishop
African Methodist Episcopal Church
Baltimore, Maryland, U.S.A.
June 2017

...

Foreword II

To be granted the privilege of writing the Foreword to *Preaching While Bleeding*, is a testament to a friendship that has endured from the early 1980s until now. My friendship with H. Beecher Hicks, Jr., is a sacrament in my life. He is to me mentor, role model, counselor, and at last, Pastor. He has been and remains an invaluable source of inspiration and instruction in my preaching and pastoral journey.

It is indeed rare when one lives to witness his name take on the air of legend. This is all the more significant when one has to first emerge from a brilliant and stellar background. Not only is Dr. Hicks a third-generation preacher, bearing the family name of high distinction, he has the unique legacy of maternal and paternal grandparents who were college graduates, this at a time when such educational attainments were rare given the social history of the United States regarding African Americans. Out of this background, Dr. Hicks has emerged as one of the greatest preachers in the history of this republic, a faithful and visionary pastor, able administrator, distinguished educator, respected scholar, Christian statesman, and prolific writer. From his own pen we are once again the beneficiaries of his towering intellect, passionate heart, and more than half a century of excellence in ministry to the Lord Christ and His people.

Preaching While Bleeding is an essential and necessary word in due season for those practitioners of the craft who take preaching seriously, as well as those who listen to preaching or those who regard preaching as an anachronism, no longer useful but not yet to be discarded. The message of this book arrives at a time of religious ambiguity, and moral relativism coupled with social and political dislocations that have left us all but paralyzed with uncertainty. This significant work is a primer for the preacher at the beginning of the journey, a source of direction and encouragement for those bearing the burden in light of common day, and a word of assurance and comfort for those long at the task while yet giving witness to "fire shut up in their bones."

With an uncanny style and surgical precision, Dr. Hicks accurately analyzed the perplexing conundrums within and without the church. He has dared to disturb us with difficult questions, forced us to deal with our humanity in all its grandeur and grime, to revisit our call and conviction, while locating our position as preacher, priest, pastor, and prophet. To read this work is to struggle with relevance and significance in a world of rapid change while anchoring securely in the timely and timeless Word of God.

All who read this book, take seriously its admonitions, and prayerfully heed its sage counsel, will find renewed purpose and power in the highest and holiest of all human endeavors. This work forces us to face the uncomfortable realities of our contemporary situation by challenging, disturbing, and even rebuking our false, often comfortable, albeit meaningless assumptions and traditions.

Finally, one cannot read this volume and not be confronted by the unmistakable and sometimes painful stains of "blood" on every page. This is not a cold, detached theoretical dissertation written by a sheltered academician removed from the harsh "bloody" realities of our human existence. An eminently prominent preacher, Dr. Hicks has demonstrated for us in his own life and labors work and witness how to weather the violent tempest and labor under insuperable burdens. His magnificent preaching and writing is soaked in blood. From him and with him, we come face to face with the pain predicament and that joy - sorrow motif that rests at the heart of authentic preaching.

"Preaching While Bleeding" allows us to come to grips with disconcerting reality that there can be no preaching without bleeding. Though we "lustily" sing that old song, "There is power in the blood," we go forth to preach calling to mind the words of John Henry Jowett, "when we bleed, we bless!"

BISHOP J. DOUGLAS WILEY TAYLOR
Life Center Cathedral
New Orleans, Louisiana
June 2017

. . .

Introduction

Thoughts On Preaching

I am a Preacher. At least that is what I've been trying to be. I could not avoid it, or escape it actually. I believe it was sealed into my DNA. Somehow destiny was wrapped up in my name and defined my being by it. My middle name secured it. Lyman Beecher, an anti-slavery preacher. Henry Ward Beecher, a Congregational preacher, known to purchase the freedom of slaves with coins from his own purse. Before I was born, I would be nothing more, nothing less than a Preacher.

William Hicks was a preacher. My grandfather was born just days after President Abraham Lincoln signed the *Emancipation Proclamation* to provide for the freedom of the nation's slaves. Perhaps in a plantation's shanty, or down by some riverside, William Hicks was set apart to be a preacher. I never knew my grandfather to wear anything other than a Black suit, a black tie, white shirt and high-top shoes with eyelets at the top, morning, noon, and night. And of course, the ever present "long-johns." Whenever you saw him you were looking at a sho-nuff preacher, a Preacher's Preacher. And he never died. He cheated death. He just slipped away on a Sunday morning when no one was looking and, as he said, *"I have to go off to save the world!"*

Henry Beecher Hicks, Sr., my father, was a preacher. Born amid the sweltering Alabama heat, it seemed nothing could escape his energy, his determination to make his mark on the world. Family legend has it that as a lad he was so interested in visiting churches to hear the preaching, his parents, William and Olivia, had to devise strategies to keep their aggressive, talkative son at home. The day came when they resorted to the unfortunate strategy of making young Henry wear a girl's dress, thinking of course, that he would stay at home if for no reason other than shame. Determined to have his way, the next time they saw Henry was atop a horse-drawn hearse that passed nearby and he was merrily on his way to church still attired in that dress. By the time of his departure he was known as *"The Pontiff"* or *"The Prophet of Main Street,"* a tribute to his pastoral years at his beloved Mount Olivet Church on Main Street in Columbus, Ohio.

Ivan Douglas Hicks, my youngest son, is a preacher; the son of a preacher, who is the son of a preacher. Ivan is the fourth generation sent by God. He, too, is blessed with the burden of the "Preacher" designation.

However, he has surpassed us all; pastor, an academic scholar in the field of Afrocentric studies, social activist, community leader and educator, possessed of rare and special gifts. When his final page is written, however, his biographer will call him a "Preacher."

These words, of course, are intended as an introduction for the reader to know my roots, my history, my heritage, and my hope. They seek to adequately shape the scope and context of what for me has been the engagement of my life and time on Mother Earth. To be a preacher is all I know to do and all I have known to do. I have desired or pursued nothing else. Entering the twilight years of my life, now that I have received three more years than David's estimate of *"three score years and ten,"* in the words of Dr. Charles Edward Booth, I have now asked God for "overtime." Enough overtime, to be sure, to write these few words and to share with those who shall read them my thoughts along my journey—thoughts that come from a life fully invested in the pastorate and in preaching the glorious Gospel of Jesus Christ, to structure, to approach in some systematic way the reason for my being and for my commitment to this all-consuming task.

Greater still, this writing will seek to make sense of the necessity so many find to approach others with the audacious assumption that any of us have the moral authority to speak to the people of God on behalf of God or, most especially, that the words that fall from our lips are, indeed, the Words of God. What chutzpah!

The question with which I must personally wrestle, if indeed I am a preacher, is whether or not I have done anything to be worthy of the title I claim.

This writing is important to me, quite frankly, because it permits me to share my "journey" in the context of the preaching/pastoral discipline which has defined my life and defined who I am as well. It has not always been easy; to be sure there have been high moments, astounding victories, aggravating defeats, and abundant blessings. For thirty-seven years I have been kept in the sheltering love of a patient congregation whose loyalty and faithfulness astound me still.

Week by week, it was my lot to climb preaching stairs on days when clouds hovered low; I preached even when dreams and visions were laid waste. I preached through seasons of storm and seasons of personal pain and struggle. My preaching, though, had blood on it. It was a preacher's blood; my blood. Nevertheless, through a strange process of pastoral empathy, I cried when my people bled; my people cried when they watched me bleed. After the waste of the years, strangely but surely, we had become one.

There is danger, of course, in this type of confessional transparency. It might be better for me and for others were I to take the advice given to one Jonathan in the Book of Judges: *"Hold thy peace, lay thy hand upon thy mouth, and go with us." (Judges 18: 3-4, 18)*

It seems reasonable, I think, to ask some hard and uncomfortable questions. Who am I and why am I in this space? What is this non-sense I hear when some say they are "Called"? Who is calling? Why are they calling? What are these mysterious, unexplainable nocturnal "urges" to preach of which they speak?

Does God use an I-Phone? Does an omniscient God require the use of a "smart phone"? If God answers prayer, does God use *Twitter?* Or, perhaps send pictures by *Snapchat?* Or should each of the 66 Books of the Bible have their own YouTube channel? Is this preaching business nothing more than the proud illusions of a loquacious ego?

As we preach from dusty, undecipherable and ancient texts, how reliable and relevant are their claims for those who worship (or not) in a twenty-first century culture? Has worship unfortunately been replaced by "Live Streaming"? Is the church and, therefore, is our preaching still valid? Was it ever? Or is it still necessary? Or would God be better off to just use *Facebook Live* and instantly, dramatically multiply the capacities of constant contact?

To pose the larger doctrinal question, could it be that God has designed something new, something different, something more dynamic and promising that will take the place of preaching? Is God about to unveil some "new thing," some new wine for old wineskins that will be more acceptable to Millennials, NextGeners' or other such demographic interest's groups. If so, what will the new "branding" of the preacher look like, sound like, preach like?

Will our preaching help to resolve or intensify the chaos?

Will our preaching advance community or will preachers remain silent or mute amid the conflicts, permitting rocks to cry out, taking our place?

Will there be some fresh voice of righteousness that will be heard above the din of a world insistent on its own will, insistent on culture rather than Christ, insistent on obeying human laws rather than God's?

Will our weekly sermonic exercises amount to a "hand over our mouths" and tongues that are still, while the flag flies higher than the cross?

Will the words we preach be the balm or the bane of our existence?

Will this new brand of preaching be offered with power and conviction, with power to change society, its purposes and priorities and all who live within it; or shall we be left to preach chained to our lectionaries, with tired sermons, rehearsed and memorized, preached to sleeping and comatose congregations who are no longer awakened to the sounds of tarnished brass and disquieted cymbals?

> *"Cry aloud, spare not, lift up thy voice,*
> *and shew my people their transgressions,*
> *and the House of Jacob their sins!"*
> ISAIAH 58:1

Remember: *"Where a trumpet is expected a flute will not suffice!"*

Maybe the most searing and relevant question about our preaching is this: **Is anybody listening?** Is anybody hearing? Does anybody really care what or if we preach at all? If the answers we hear are in the negative, then the only question that remains is: *Why bother?* The questions we must approach are insistent and demand response.

I welcome the reader into my world of preaching, prophetic preaching, homiletics, and beyond. You may find this writing too "preachy" from time to time. You should not be surprised. Being "too preachy" is an occupational hazard. I will rely on an abundant sufficiency of your grace.

Hopefully, this writing will confront you, and challenge to deeper thought regarding God, Jesus, the Church and its preaching and, of course, your role and place within it. You may be uncomfortable with my positions. You may challenge my assumptions and presuppositions. This writing may anger you and ask demanding questions of you. You may even choose to put this book aside and let it collect dust on your bookshelf. That is, as it should be, a part of the process. It is also my hope that in the end there will be a clearer view of who we are and what God demands of us as God's disciples and as spokespersons for the Living God. So, I ask you. What does God require of you?

> "So here's what I want you to do. God helping you: Take your everyday, ordinary life—your sleeping, eating, going-to-work and walking around life—and place it before God as an offering. Embracing what

*God does for you is the best thing you can do for Him.
Don't become so well-adjusted to your culture that
you fit into
it without even thinking. Instead, fix your attention
on God. You'll be changed from the inside out.
Readily recognize what God wants from you and
respond to it. Unlike the culture around you, always
dragging you down to its level of immaturity,
God brings the best out of you,
develops well-formed maturity in you."*
(ROMANS 12:1-2 THE MESSAGE)

Nothing more; nothing less!

Thoughts on Bleeding and the Blood:
A Necessary Preface

It was a sticky, hot night in Alabama. I do not remember the name of the town. I'm not even sure that the town had a name. All I can remember is that I was somewhere in Alabama, the dirt road veered off from Highway 80E, the highway infamously remembered for the March across a bridge on a Sunday called "Bloody." The bridge, of course, was named for a General in the Confederate Army and, in addition, he became famous for his position as Grand Dragon of the Ku Klux Klan and later a United States Senator from the state of Alabama. On this night, however, I was in a car with Reverend Isaac C. Acoff, Pastor of the Bethel Hill Missionary Baptist Church at Marengo County, Alabama; a church erected in 1894. We were on our way to church.

The dirt and gravel road made it a frightening journey along the unlit narrow path. Rev. Acoff talked while I prayed. This was an experience for which I was wholly unprepared. We were headed for the church he served only two Sundays a month and I was to be the guest preacher for five nights during the month of August. They called it a "Lay-by Revival," held while the field workers waited for their crops to be ripe and ready for the harvest. At the time, I don't think I had five sermons to my name but I was "bent, bound, and determined" to do the best I could.

Upon arrival we were greeted by all ten of the membership, the singing of Long and Common meter hymns was well underway. It seemed everyone had their personal "funeral home" fan to keep the breeze flowing and the mosquitoes from biting necks. However, by evening's end, a great time was had by all.

It soon came to dawn on me that there was something singular and significant about these persons for whom I had been called to preach. These were laborers of the field; they were the descendants of slaves and sharecroppers who tilled the soil and harvested the crop, and put food on tables from which they could never eat, and made up beds on which they would never sleep. Their blood was literally in the earth in which they planted, the soil from which they would so meagerly share.

While there I could not forget Selma. I found my wife in Selma and that was the best thing I could say about that southern city. There would be blood on the bridge at Selma; on Sunday, blood from policemen's whips, blood from horse's hoofs, blood sanctioned by the state. And still there we were in the deepest region of the South, in the woods, in the heat, in worship, remembering the blood. All they had, all they owned was a Bible; a worn-out book that taught them about the blood. There was blood enough on those crowded ships of the Middle Passage. There was blood enough on auction blocks where mothers and fathers, sisters and brothers were sold and divided to live their days in plantation fields. And when women dropped their babies in the soil beneath cotton plants, there in the birthing sun there was blood. They understood the blood, they preached the blood, and all they knew was, despite their circumstance, strangely they sang, "there is power, wonder working power in the blood." I hear their voices still.

> "O de blood, O de blood,
> the blood done signed my name."
>
> Ain't you glad; ain't you glad,
> The blood done signed your name?
>
> Hallelujah, thank You Jesus,
> The blood done signed my name."

Over and over they sang the refrain until it seemed that heaven's choir had joined the singing. And I knew then, before I preached a word, indeed the blood had signed *my* name.

Forgive my redundancy. This is a word that must be heard: If you preach, you will bleed. In your ministry you will be taken to the deepest regions of human hurt, you will be taken to those highways of crushed humanity where blood will be spilled without reason, you will be called upon to preach a healing message to those who bleed before your very eyes; but most importantly you will be called upon to preach while your own blood seeps out through the broken vessels of your life and spills beneath your preaching robes to saturate the very floor upon which you stand.

Preaching while bleeding? The very thought sends a frigid shiver through the soul.

Preaching while bleeding? Perhaps you are not preaching if you are not bleeding.

Bleeding is your necessary gift.

Bleeding is your necessary sacrifice.

Bleeding is your gift of honor.

Bleeding—as in Adam's rib, extracted in the bloody flow from his internal organs.

Bleeding—as in Moses and the blood spread on the doorposts at Goshen.

Bleeding—as in the blood extracted from Jacob's hip replacement that night he went out toward that place called Bethel, only to come away with a bloody limp.

God calls you to preach for those who bleed.

Still there is more. God calls you to know the privilege of bleeding personally.

The One who calls on Mary to bleed in the sacrifice of child bearing, calls upon you to bleed as well.

The One who calls on that nameless woman to bleed for twelve years of menstruation calls upon you to bleed, even when you dare not ask why.

The One who calls on you to bleed as did Paul, pierced by a thorn in your side, will permit you to bleed when the only available cure is His all sufficient grace.

There can be no preaching that does not simultaneously offer judgment for our yesterdays but redemption and hope for future tomorrows.

There can be no preaching that does not cause one to bleed for others and no blood that will not empower the preaching that "reaches to the highest mountain and flows to the lowest valley." All sermons are mere words caught in the high weeds of irrelevance unless and until that sermon has some blood on it.

When the One who suffered, bled, and died on Calvary looks down upon you from His Cross, the only question that remains is this: can you preach knowing that His blood is spilled, while it should be yours? Or will you share with Him this incredible, inescapable assignment: preach if you will, prophesy if you must, but be assured that as you preach you will bleed.

The Authority of Scripture

> Jesus Loves Me, This I know,
> For the Bible tells me so.
> Little ones to Him belong,
> They are weak but He is strong!

Any dialogue with regard to the matter of preaching must begin with the notion of Scripture and its authority. As the lyric from the children's hymn tells us, the truth we seek and the truth that sustains is found in the Bible, the source of such truth. "The Bible tells me so!" That's the end of the discussion. That's it. That's all.

One doctrinal writer has written that "the Bible is a book written under the divine inspiration of God and accepted by Christians as the Word of God," and, there is a "proof text" to go along with it. *"All Scripture is given by inspiration of God, and is profitable for doctrine, for reproof, for correction, for instruction in righteousness: that the man (woman)[6] of God may be perfect, thoroughly furnished unto all good works."* (II Tim. 3:16, 17)

A broader and I think more acceptable statement of this case is written by Drs. Martha Simmons and Frank A. Thomas in their introductory comments in *Preaching with Sacred Fire*. They state:

> "When we consider the Black (primarily Christian) preaching tradition, several principles emerge. The first is the centrality of the Bible. This is not to

---

6   Parenthesis mine.

> be taken for rigid literalism; the Bible is seen as an inspired and dynamic source for understanding the world and as a wise guide for life's decisions.
>
> Dr. Cleophus J. LaRue states: "Indeed, it is no secret that the Bible occupies a central place in the religious life of Black Americans. More than a source for texts, in Black preaching the Bible is the single most important source of language, imagery, and story for the sermon." [7]

That the Bible is authoritative and its teachings are to be followed was accompanied by the fact that its laws were observed. This is a central part of what we learned as children in Sunday School. In Sunday School we learned of something called *"inerrancy"* and *"infallibility."* In the world of our parents the whole of Scripture was accepted as truth just as it was written—verbatim, "truth without any mixture of error" they called it; and it was to be normative for our lives.

It would not be long, however, before many considered such a blanket acceptance as thoughtless if not naïve. It would not be long before we would ask searching questions regarding the "sacredness" of Scripture in comparison with any other "spiritual" writings.

An unholy romance with agnosticism and atheism has risen among us. In contemporary culture the church, the Bible and our preaching appear to be suddenly, hopelessly, irrelevant. There are not too many

---

[7] Martha Simmons and Frank A. Thomas, Preaching with Sacred Fire, W. W. Norton and Company, New York, 2010, p. 7.

churches around these days with Bible Study overflowing. Does anyone really believe Scripture anymore? It would not be long before our culture would be in search of a "new normal."

From my point of view, that "new normal" would be found in our understanding of who we were as a consequence of our condition of Blackness and the critical and criminal circumstance of slavery through which we had come. The Bible could be normative for us to the extent that we found our condition and our hope in the context of the biblical narrative. When writing of the development of Negro spirituals as discussed by Dr. Allen Callahan, he joins Cheryl Kirk-Duggan with the suggestion that the spirituals are *"an early, unique form that rereads biblical texts."* It was in this manner that *"the slaves read their experience into and out of the Bible."*

My suggestion is not that the Bible is not authoritative, nor that it should be viewed in any manner as wholly literal. Rather I am contending that the Bible is authoritative to the extent that it speaks to my circumstance, empowers my escape from life's painful encounters, empowers me to overcome the assault of the enemy, provides hope for my future, joy for my journey and insists on my liberation; a liberation that is unrestrained by human interference, or unjust laws or any other force that would deny my humanity or circumscribe the me-ness of me. In other words, I am somebody. I count. I am important in the economy of God. I matter!

That is why racism based on religion is so antithetical to my understanding of Scripture. The Bible teaches that my religion must always be the bridge between my present reality and my future destiny. My understanding of Scripture is that my religion is defined or will only be limited by my actions; my transformation will be secured by my faith.

All Scripture, to be authoritative, must not save part of me, it must be available to save all of me. The Jesus of the Bible must be the Jesus that takes comfort sitting in my living room, a Jesus who "gives me all my medicine in my room." All Scripture, in order to be redemptive, must be intentionally specific and personally anticipated. It must be for me, and about me. It must, in the words of our ancestors, *"suit our case."* It is in this manner, as I am able to contextualize Scriptures in line with my own existential circumstance, that the Bible makes sense. Allen Callahan says it this way:

> *"The slaves also found that while they yet awaited complete deliverance they could be sustained against all odds and in impossible circumstances:*
>
> *God delivered Daniel from the mouth of the lion and from the hand of man; the slaves then asked rhetorically, Why not every man?"* [8]

Callahan goes further to say, *"It was under the American slavery regime that African Americans learned to read*

---

8   Ibid, p. 29.

the Bible into their lives. They also learned to read their lives into the Bible."⁹

> *I Believe I'll Testify ...*
>
> "The prophetic theology of the Black Church during the days of chattel slavery was a theology of liberation. It was preached to set free those who were held in bondage (spiritually, psychologically, and sometimes physically) and it was practiced to set the slaveholders free from the notion that they could define other human beings or confine a soul set free by the power of the Gospel."
>
> JEREMIAH WRIGHT
> Lecture, Colgate Rochester Crozier Theological Seminary, 2014

I am, then, a Bible-based preacher. And let me say quite clearly, lest there be any confusion; I am not a writer who preaches, I am a preacher who writes. In my hands as, Sunday by Sunday, I mount the pulpit, I am holding a King James Version of the Bible, complete with all the Elizabethan English I can command. (Some habits are hard to break!!) I read it, however, with a twist. I read it, as suggested by a Swedish theologian known as the most important Christian theologian of the 20th century, Karl Barth, who said: I go to the pulpit with *"the Bible in one hand and the newspaper in the other."* Barth went further to say, "The Pastor and the Faithful should not deceive themselves into thinking that they are a religious society, which has to do

---

9   Ibid, p. 29.

with certain themes; they live in the world. We still need—according to my old formulation—the Bible and the Newspaper." [10]

Yet, I do not shy away from the latest version or the newest translation of Scripture. No matter the version, I'll just take my newspaper with me. It's all God's Word and if it helps to make me a faithful interpreter of that Word, "rightly dividing the Word of truth," I want to read and absorb it in every form available to me. Let there be no confusion: *"The grass withereth, the flower fadeth, but the Word of our God shall stand forever!"* (Isa. 40:8)

Theology Before Methodology

The a'priori question to consider before anyone preaches is, *"Who is God?"* It is the question of all theology—or God-knowledge. *Who is God? What is God to you? Do you know God? Does God know you? What is your relationship with God? Is it fleeting or full? Is it intimate or casual? Can you trust God? Can God trust you?*

Long before one can safely ask the question, "How shall I preach?" one must first deal with the question, "Do you know the One of whom you preach?" or, "Do you know God?" The "Who" must come before the "How." After all, whether you are an impromptu preacher, an expository preacher, or a manuscript preacher, it won't

---

10 Nacreous Kingdom Blogspot. com, October 22, 2010.

make a difference if you have no knowledge of the God about whom you are to preach.

The principle is a simple one: One can speak only of that which one knows. Anything else will ring hollow, false, and untrue. Anything else will not pass the integrity test and will be seen as the product of the hypocrisy that it is.

I want to be sure, as the underlying philosophical principle of this book, that the reader and the preacher, the saint or the sinner, can answer these questions: Do you know who God is? Do you know what God does? Do you know how God acts in human history? These are the questions that the Bible seeks to answer from Genesis to Revelation, no matter where you start, no matter where you stop. I am not suggesting that the preacher must know the answer to these questions before preaching; rather, that there must be a significant wrestling, intellectual engagement, and spiritual grappling that takes place prior to engagement with preaching and ministry. I simply suggest before you preach that you seek to find the answer to these questions as they will shape and mold the preacher/prophet you are to become.

Just a few small, pithy questions, I tell you. Yet they are filled with meaning and implication. These questions must be answered. The preacher who cannot handle these questions adequately will know immediately that he or she suffers from a serious GDS (God-deficiency Syndrome). Such a deficiency will be obvious and quickly detected by others. The deficiency will be noted in anemic sermons, an unsatisfactory or non-existent prayer life, an inability to be with others with transparency, an absence of faith, as well as a persistent struggle with anxiety and self-doubt. The world will never be sure whether they are really Saints or merely showmen.

Ernest Burrell was the oldest living Deacon on the Board of the small church I pastored in Upstate New York. I made a hospital visit to see him as the report had come that he was "low sick!" That was just the local way of saying he was seriously ill and was not expected to live much longer. When I found him the nurse reported to me that he was unresponsive and had not spoken for many days. At an age of nearly 100 years, what else could one expect? As I stood over his bed, his face to the wall, he remained unmoved and silent. Undeterred, I called his name. "Deacon Burrell." Once. Twice. And then he moved, slowly turning in his bed to see his visitor. Old Deacon Burrell looked me squarely in the eye and said, "Reverend, you can't make me doubt Him! I know too much about Him!" I shouted all the way home. Deacon Burrell had a story to tell and even on death's bed he didn't mind telling it!

The pure essence of preaching has to do with the telling of a story. First and foremost, the story we are to tell is the story of Jesus who is the Christ. No matter where your story begins, no matter where it ends, it must present to the listener the great claims of the Gospel. Your story must be the great story, the great watchwords of our faith. Preach to me and tell me who God is. Preach to me and tell me the great creation story. Tell me of Noah and his Ark, of Abraham and his ram, of Moses and his bush. Preach to me and tell me of God's Covenants as well as God's Commandments. Preach to me and tell me of a birth in Bethlehem, a crucifixion on Friday and a resurrection on Sunday. And when you preach, teach. Teach me of grace and mercy. Teach me of Sanctification and Justification, teach me of healing and hope, of the new birth and life Everlasting. Teach me Good News!

Such a simple thing. Tell the story. And you must tell the story in such a way that those who hear it will see themselves in it. In fact, you must tell it until you see yourself in it. Yours will not always be a pretty story. It is not always a comfortable story but as long as it is *your* story, it is a *necessary* story. It may be a story that dredges up old guilt, or reminds you of yesterday's sin. But preach until you convert yourself. Preach until you can't stand yourself. And the folk who come to hear you preach, if you preach a sermon of conviction, will not want to hear you anymore but they'll come back next Sunday because they love to hear that story! They'll come back saying, "where is that Preaching Man/Woman."

Still it is the kind of story, the more you tell it the more you have to tell it. It remains your story, the story that reveals something of your situation, that reveals with transparency the authenticity of your faith, the story of your loss and your gain; of being lost and found, of being empty and filled. It's the thrill of your victories; the agony of your defeats. It's the stuff of preaching. It's the living illustration you will never find in textbook or commentary, never to be found on the Internet. It makes preaching memorable and powerful, even as it makes praise glorious! Tell the story!

Yet, it is not the telling of *any* story, a cause for a personal pity party, or an excuse to feel sorry for yourself; it is the telling of *your* story in relationship to *your* experience and *your* knowledge of the Eternal. It is the story of Christ you are telling but it is empowered for preaching; a gift of the Holy Spirit that as you preach to yourself so you will be able to peek into the lives of your listeners and speak a word that is redemptive and salvific. And the pew may never want to hear you again but if you are faithful to this Word, on the way out the side sanctuary door, you will hear somebody say: "He doesn't know me that well; she can't talk to me like that." And, believe it or not that's Good News!

Perhaps you do not find it easy to tell a story about your life or to be so introspective that you can sense the sacred task of addressing the lives of others and in so doing come to meet yourself in the sermon.

Still, anyone can tell a story about their life—your first car, your first love, your first kiss, your first job, and all the funny stories which accompany those topics.

Your story need not be a sermon. Told from an intensely personal space your story will become your sermon without help from you. So, then, tell your story in relationship to the God you know. Can you tell the story in relationship to the One who is your hope and your health, your life and your salvation? Can you tell your story and tell how your life was altered, your home was blessed, your outlook was changed, your marriage was enriched? Because of the lines of your story you are required to say, *"He's done so much for me I cannot tell it all."*

Tell that story and someone will accuse you of preaching! Tell that story and someone will believe that you know the Lord for yourself. Tell someone that story and the world will soon believe that in their lives rocks can move, stones can roll away, resurrection is real and no matter how deep the grave there yet remains a way to get out alive! Tell that story and men and women will come to know that the Bible is real, relevant, and authoritative for their lives. Tell that story and you will have the matter in the right order, theology before methodology.

Three Seminarians:
Meaning, Relevance, and Will It Preach?

Granville Seward is my friend. He has been my friend for more than fifty years. I have dined at his dinner table and shared time with his children. I have watched him through the shifting seasons of life, from the days of joy when his children were born, to that fateful day when he laid his wife tenderly to rest. I found excited sleep in his home the night my wife, Elizabeth, gave birth to our first-born son, Henry III. In every sense, Granville and I have been friends.

We came to know each other best, however, during our time together as theologs at Colgate Rochester Divinity School. Granville and I, "homies" from Columbus, Ohio, were two of three Black students admitted to CRDS in the fall of 1964. The three of us, including Wilson Fallin from Birmingham, Alabama, comprised the "quota" of African Americans that could be admitted in one academic year. For three years, Granville, Wilson and I would have the same course curriculum, the same professors, the same assignments and, quite often, the same grades. Destiny made us brothers; history, racism, and necessity made us friends.

More to the point, the three of us shared a relationship born in the halls of our venerable seminary. For it was within her walls, up and down her hallways, in the Refectory and out on the "hill," that we learned real preaching skills by methods that were not taught in the classroom. In many ways we used each other as Guinee pigs for the practice of our preaching. I guess we kind of taught ourselves. Therein, as the saying goes, lies a tale!

Granville was the one among us who took great delight in describing the differences and similarities that we shared. On surface, Granville was a country boy, fresh from a hamlet called "Rendville," a rural community in south eastern Ohio. Because he was the oldest of the three it naturally fell to him to be concerned about Wilson and me, much as a father looks after his sons. Many were the days when we stumbled into chapel together, anxious to hear what astounding and challenging preaching would fall from the lips of the school President, Gene E. Bartlett. He could not *"whoop,"* but we were agreed, the man could preach.

Differences

Granville frequently rehearsed our differences. Granville described himself as philosopher / theologian / thinker. Granville was quite at ease in dialogue with historic classical theologians, Bultmann, Heidegger, Barth, Tillich and the rest. Granville could never live an "unexamined life." He wanted to be transparent and to insist that others were the same. He gave serious thought to the matters of the day and was always caught in a conversation about "meaning." No matter what one said or what the circumstance one faced, his first response was always to ask, "What does it mean?"

Wilson Fallin, however, was the one of the trilogy who hailed from the steel community of Bessemer, Alabama, just a stone's throw from Birmingham, Alabama, Theophilus Eugene "Bull" Connor, George Wallace, the land of Jim Clark, Fred Shuttlesworth, Martin Luther King, and all the cast of characters from the deeply divided and segregated South. Wilson was the radical among us; the social activist before the term was born.

Wilson was the historian, the one who would examine the events of the nation in light of historic trends and the social demands voiced by African Americans.

We remember Wilson most especially for that day in our first course in Old Testament. Dr. James Alvin Sanders, a brilliant, internationally renowned scholar, was lecturing on some obscure Old Testament point when, tiring of the process, Wilson raised his hand to question the professor:

> Wilson: "Dr. Sanders when are you going to make this Old Testament relevant?"

To quote the Book of Revelation, *"There was silence in heaven about the space of half an hour!"* (Rev. 8:1)

Most of us thought it but were too cowardly, too craven to give those thoughts voice. Wilson, however, dared to give voice to his thoughts despite his fears and suggested that the Old Testament and, indeed, the Bible must stand up to the "relevance test" if it were to be accepted and believed. Relevance would be and was of critical importance to those who must be interpreters of the Word in the face of a generation that prayed-in, sat-in and waded-in, and marched-in. For Wilson it was all a waste of time if the Old Testament, indeed, the Bible was not relevant.

Will It Preach?

When it came to me, however, Wilson and Granville had great fun poking at me for I sought to be the preacher among them. Ol' Henry Hicks had come to seminary for only one purpose—to learn how to preach. My question among them all was this: will it preach? In light of a particular theological position, were its claims so clear, was its doctrinal leading so precise, could we take it to a pulpit on any Sunday morning and would it preach?! Would it be effective? Would it speak directly to the profound issues of life? Would it be the word that would cause a collective "Amen" and bring hope to hurting hearts? Would it provide a fresh insight on the meaning of life, wake up the pews and stimulate the choir? No matter the historic moment or the instance of societal conflict, after historical analysis and in light of theological review, the question that remains is, "will it preach?"

These three points of view are critical for the examination of this writing. Wilson Fallin is now retired as President of Birmingham Bible College after more than thirty years; Granville has retired from a successful pastorate at the Mt. Zion Church in Newark, New Jersey after thirty-five years; My tenure of thirty-seven years as Pastor of the Metropolitan Church in Washington, D. C. has come to an end. Yet, forty years later we are still asking the same questions of each other:

What Does It Mean?

As we review the substance of our preaching, as we seek clarity with the words we speak, we must never fail to ask, "what does it mean?" What does it (whatever the subject before us) mean in terms of the human predicament? How does what we think and how we approach the interior conflicts and battles of our lives contribute to a sense of value and meaning that make life worth living? In a time of rejection for the institutional church and disaffection with organized religion, what does it mean when some theologian rises to lecture on a God of "Ultimate Concern" or seeks to point us to a God who is "wholly Other"?

In a time of political turmoil and shifting political alliances, when profane men take upon themselves the task of making *"America Great Again,"* what does it mean to preach instead that *"the government shall be upon God's shoulders?"* In a time of anxious fears and rising doubts, how do I apply the message of the Gospel to my existential situation? In a time of racial unrest, what does it mean to preach of a "beloved community" or to shout into the wind "Black Lives Matter," sensing all the while that no one really cares? Or so it seems. I ask again, what does it mean?

How Relevant Is It?

Take this for a suggestion: the next time you approach the pulpit for your weekly foray in the chosen text for the day, stop for a moment and ask this question: How relevant is it? In light of what my congregation faces, in light of the headlines in the morning newspaper or the lead story on CNN, in the face of some politician who suggests something completely left of center and wants to build a wall to shut the world out, or when you must acknowledge the deeply disturbing news a doctor gave to the woman seated on the third row to the right, in terms of what you came to say, in light of your sophomoric interpretation of scripture, how relevant is it?

This Word we preach must have meaning as well as relevance if it is to be life giving, life sustaining, and soul redeeming. The new preacher **must** come to understand that what is important is not *what you say* but *how what you say was heard*. Brilliant speech and soaring oratory will never replace straight-forward, down-to-earth preaching that touches the heart and saves the soul. And that is why we are compelled to ask of the exegetical opportunities of life: **WILL IT PREACH?** And Chapel at Colgate Rochester had not come to a successful climax until the entire assembly of students lifted their voices in all four verses of "Unto the Hills Around Do I Lift Up!"

Every word that is written with elegance and eloquence will not preach. Every sermon that is offered with Pentecostal power may not be God-kissed or God ordained. If not, it will not preach.

Every sermon that is offered with human thinking or human intelligence, may not necessarily preach. Every torn and tattered homily may not deserve to be given voice simply because in the congregation of human hurt and broken hearts, it will not preach.

Preaching is hard enough, difficult enough, demanding enough when it is supported by both meaning and relevance; it becomes all the more difficult, however, when the offering of some Sunday morning is dead before it begins because it is not supported by prayer, it is not under-pinned by spiritual discipline and sustained by the sure knowledge that, in the end, God alone must do the preaching. If not, it will not preach.

Granville, Wilson and I have all retired now, but not quite. Truth be told, while we are no longer in the "active" pastorate we are still somewhere trying to "sneak a preach" every chance we get. Still, we know this: Authentic preaching will require blood. Preaching is about life. Life is in the blood. Every old preacher knows and every young preacher sooner or later will learn, that authentic preaching requires blood—some pastoral pain, some anxious fear, some painful rebuke, some careless accusation—a requirement for blood; drawn, perhaps, from Emmanuel's veins and mine.

It is a part of the process. You will preach while you bleed. Trust me. Any preaching that has meaning and relevance will ultimately have blood on it. It is to this reality we now turn.

> *Temptations, hidden snares*
> *Often take us unawares,*
> *And our hearts are made to bleed*
> *For some thoughtless word or deed.*
> *And we wonder why the test*
> *When we try to do our best,*
> *But we'll understand it better*
> *By and by!* [11]

---

[11] https://hymnary.org/text/we_are_tossed_and_driven_on_the_restless.

.1.

Preaching Matters!

I was struck most recently by a writing by Dr. Timothy Keller of Redeemer Presbyterian Church in New York. Dr. Keller simply titles his work *Preaching*, but adds to it this additional tag-line: *Communicating Faith in an Age of Skepticism*.[12]

Dr. Keller is correct. This is an age of skepticism. Yet it is more. This is also an age of pessimism, cynicism, and humanism; an age of nagging doubts and stubborn questions. This is an age when old truths have given way to immorality and the destruction of sacred human life. The "rules" no longer apply. Civility is a thing of the past. The gathering we call the "church" and those who preach within it are viewed with suspicion, mere keepers of religious antiquities who have no purpose in this new age.

---

12   Keller, Timothy. Preaching. Viking Random House, New York, NY,. 2015, p/9ff.

It's not your Daddy's *Buick* anymore. It's a *Tesla* now, and it runs on batteries and not by gas. This is an era when the principles upon which our nation was founded have come under attack and the church is no longer regarded as the bearer of eternal truths. Her pulpits are no longer regarded by the intellectual and spiritual giants we once knew in our storied ecclesiastical past.

Such was the context of my recent teaching engagement with students at a local Protestant seminary. They had literally come from the length and breadth of the country; even a few from the Caribbean isles. A few were first year entering theological students but most were "Middlers" (second year) or rising Seniors. Most were bi-vocational students; work by day, Seminary by night. Nevertheless, they had enrolled, according to the registrar, for a class I was to teach titled, *"Preaching and Worship in the African American Tradition."*

This was not my first rodeo. I have taught in numerous seminaries so I was prepared for what I could expect. Or so I thought. I approached the task with energy, enthusiasm even. I was aware of the sacrifice of time and energy every student made to come for instruction for three hours a semester, an evening course.

Soon we began rounds of *preaching*. Each student, week by week, would bring a prepared sermon/homily based on a Scripture pericope of their selection. After hearing all of the students, sharing individual critiques, I began to respond, firmly but compassionately, to what I had heard and experienced.

I had questions. What in the world are we doing? Does anyone want to preach? Really? I can't tell! Does anyone have what one person called "that burning desire"? Did they come to the class to complete course requirements or to be mere spectators at the biblical side-show? The students were bright; No doubt they had academic promise but they seemed disconnected, unengaged, and, frankly bored with the process. It seemed to me that, as far as these students were concerned, when it came to preaching you could "take it or leave it." When it came to the Bible only a few had what appeared to be basic knowledge not to mention an intimate romance with the Scriptures. I sensed in these students more than ambivalence; it was more a sense of empty disconnectedness and malaise. It was mine to help them overcome the pain of it all.

I wanted to teach the students how to preach what variously might be called a "good sermon." I hastened to ask myself how one could responsibly define what a "good sermon" is exactly. Then I remembered Keller's warning:

> "... the difference between a bad sermon and a good sermon is largely located in the preachers—in their gifts and skills and in their preparation for any particular message. Understanding the biblical text, distilling a clear outline and theme, developing a persuasive argument, enriching it with poignant illustrations, metaphors, and practical examples, incisively analyzing heart motives and cultural assumptions, making specific application to real

life - all of this takes extensive labor. To prepare a sermon like this requires hours of work, and to be able to craft and present it skillfully takes years of practice."[13]

It seemed to me more than an uphill battle; this was the original *"Mission Impossible."* I did not want to mislead these students with unreasonable expectations. I wanted to introduce them to great thinkers, great orators, great preachers, some contemporary, some from years past and gone, who might become their mentors in the faith. I wanted to talk with them about preachers who are serious about their craft and to get them out of the classroom and into churches, there to hear visiting clergy who came our way, exemplars of the African American tradition of preaching we had gathered to study.

I try hard not to be negative nor to be unnecessarily pessimistic. And yet, I am pained by the church. I believe that the church, generally, is troubled; but I also believe that the African American Church, specifically, is in serious trouble. To state the matter concisely and clearly: I fear that if something that is redemptive and restorative does not occur in the African American church, its future is dismal and grim. Why, you ask? If the future of the church is to be measured by the level of commitment and enthusiasm the present generation displays toward the church then, in the words of

---

[13]   Ibid, p. 10-11.

the Apostle Paul, *"We are of all men most miserable."* (I Cor. 15:19)

> *I Believe I'll Testify ...*
>
> "The future demands that we look forward, not backward. When we refuse to orient ourselves forward, we create an idol out of the past and that is spiritually deadly because it prevents God's in-breaking and prevents any substantive future progress."
>
> DR. MARVIN A. MCMICKLE, PRESIDENT
> *Bulletin, Colgate Rochester Crozer Divinity School, Summer/Fall, 2016, p. 5*

Don't ask me; ask yourselves. Where will you find young men and women who have a genuine love for God, for the church and for the preaching of the Word? Is anyone paying attention to the decline in church attendance among African American churches? Not long ago the African American church was pointed to as the one place of stability among the Christian faith in terms of church growth. Not so today.

Since my retirement from the active pastorate I have had the occasion to visit churches of various sizes and descriptions within the African American community—mega churches, small to storefront churches, contemporary, hip-hop, academic, intellectual churches, upper class, middle class, and no class; I've been there, done that. What I have observed, in a non-scientific survey of sort, is what I have come to call a "the Graying of the Church." The hair of the church has literally turned white. In a word, the church is getting "Old!" So old, in fact, that it appears the Church has either been ignored or discounted as a meaningful agent of change or an advocate of hope within the Black community.

Perhaps, as Dr. Wyatt Tee Walker suggests, you can always know what is happening sociologically within the African American community by the songs it is singing and the story of its musical score. The songs we sing very often are long in rhythm and beat but short and shallow in terms of theology and biblical importance. Choirs, with notable exceptions, are no longer known for musical skill but for the entertainment they provide. Our singing has become repetitive. There are "Seven/Eleven Songs": We sing seven verses and then repeat eleven times! Unfortunately, the Black church is no longer looked to for leadership, for strategic planning or for moral guidance. This "graying" factor may also be observed in the quality of students who are being attracted to and maintained in the shrinking number of seminaries that should be the seed and birthing ground for the church.

Furthermore, is the contemporary attitude toward preachers and their preaching a passing phenomenon or a danger sign that must not be ignored? Just what are new preachers preaching? When they do preach, why does their preaching ring so porous and shallow? We are witnessing today a decline and decay of the focus of Black preaching that hitherto has not been seen. Significant, Bible-based, edifying, thoughtful, reflective, soaring, eloquent, oratorical and pedagogical preaching appears to be a dying art. The culture has heard enough; the world is tired of words.

Is twenty-first century preaching left only to those who are able to bring the crowd to its feet, or to leave them to count how many are "slain in the Spirit"? Is it for those whose only goal is unwarranted emotional stimulation? Must the preaching be all "gravy" and no meat? What do they hope to gain from this exercise of spiritualized calisthenics? We are in trouble.

I do not mean to suggest that all is wrong with the church. Far from it. Numerous examples abound of churches great and small that are doing a magnificent work for God. Many new, young, energetic pastors are stepping forward with new ideas, new paradigms and have become a refreshing "second wind" for formerly struggling churches who have neither wind nor fire.

It does appear, however, that traditional denominations no longer command the attention and certainly not the loyalty of today's worshippers. Within the African American community there appears to be a decided shift toward Pentecostalism and hopefully toward new models of ministry that promise to transform the church into the living entity it was intended to be. The Bible has not changed but there can be no doubt, the world around the church is changing and graying. The artifacts of our existence are shifting beneath our feet and before our eyes.

Even if we begin now to re-train a generation of preachers, how shall they preach the Gospel in a world of constant change? As the church diminishes in number, in cultural influence and in every measurement of human power, who will state the case for where we are and where we shall be in the days that are to come? What young preacher of mine or yours is ready to take over and become the voice God will use for a new age? What seminary is making plans today to raise up a new gathering of preachers and prophets, preparing them to take on Elijah's mantle with a double portion of the spirit of the living God? God grant that they are doing so now!

So, a new thought emerged as I began to teach. I wanted to help. I wanted to animate students and encourage young preachers, to lighten their hearts and to let them know that there is light at the end of the tunnel.

In the best way I knew, I promised the students with these words:

'I'm going to write a book just for you and I'll have a part of it that talks about the purpose and the priority of preaching and you. Not the "how," but the "why." Not the skill but the power.'

I wanted to encourage them to know that what they dreamed of doing and becoming, the preaching power they had heard in others, the communication skills they had witnessed in other role model preachers, all those things were not beyond their grasp. I wanted them to understand, in the words of H. Richard Niebuhr, that it is possible to remain true to Christ in a materialistic age. The ancestors are leaning far out over the battlements of glory, cheering for you to make it in. In other words, you can make it! You can do it!

Maybe that's where you are. That may be where the reader of this volume is right now. It could be you have dreams of preaching, or you have seen something in others that you long to see in yourself, or observed some powerful witness in someone who has been for you a silent but effective role model. If, indeed, that is the case then this book is for you. You can make it. You can do it! I am writing the book just as I promised. Let's get to it.

The foundation for my thought is this: **PREACHING MATTERS!** I shall discuss further on the socio/spiritual implications for the **BLACK LIVES MATTER!** mantra that has empowered a new movement for the reform of the criminal justice system in America. At this juncture, however, I use the phrase in a manner that is in no way intended to be threatening, frightening, or tangential to the theme of this book.

Nevertheless, it is important to say that preaching still matters. In my view, if ever there were a moment in the history of humankind when sound, solid, redemptive preaching was required, that moment is now. This is a great time to preach!

There is no doubt that these are unprecedented times which pose a *"clear and present danger"* to the longevity of our democracy. This is a mind-boggling time when our politics are based not on hope but on anger, hatred, distrust, and paranoia. If we are not careful we will filibuster our national democracy out of existence. The tragedy, of course, is that the nation appears to be looking to the state to provide a solution for our thorniest problems and our deepest fears. We know that the nation is struggling and that change is inevitable. We just do not know the forms that change will take. Still, I insist, this is a great time for the preaching of the Gospel.

Yet, to be quite candid, we are also standing at the cross-roads of a dilemma that is the underlying problem with the matter of preaching. Let's state it this way: The Gospel, the *Kerygma* must always be proclaimed. We are, we believe, "called" to preach; and from that call there can be no escape. Paul says it quite succinctly: "How shall they then call on Him in whom they have not believed? And how shall they believe in Him of whom they have not heard? And how shall they hear without a preacher? And how shall they preach except they be sent?" (Rom. 10:14-15)

So, I am not where I am by accident. Someone had to teach me, by precept and example, what it means to preach. No matter where we are on our journey we all have a continuing need for teachers. Perhaps not in a formal sense, but preacher-teachers nonetheless. When I look back on the years of my beginnings my mind is flooded with the faces of the Saints in the Mount Olivet Church in Columbus, Ohio: Myrtle Wills, Helen Green, and James Walker, all gone now to be with the Lord. They did not boast of their formal education; no degrees adorned their walls. A few of my early teachers could hardly sign their names. But they took it as their appointed duty to mentor me, and correct me, and discipline me with a kind of *"tough love"* so that I could have the opportunity to explore the depths of the gracious gifts that God had in store for me. They were my teachers.

One wonders, however, just how this preached Gospel can attach itself meaningfully to the lives of the present culture. What word can be uttered from the pulpit that will thrive and grow on the cutting edge of this secular society that will meet the requirements of relevance?

Preaching is important; Preaching Matters. I suggest that this is the ripe moment of history when we must reclaim the pulpit. There are those who will take anything to the pulpit and call it a sermon; when in fact it is everything but a sermon. I'm an old preacher so cut me some slack! I do not know when or how it happened but someone has taken our pulpits and put them on the back-porch of theological and homiletic excellence. In addition to relevance and meaning we have lost the poetry, the rhythm, the urgent eloquence of preaching. We are told there is no longer reason or warrant to preach for conviction, confession or conversion. This is not reality TV. The eternal souls of those who are before us are at stake. Yet, we have permitted the culture to rob us of our pulpits; they have soiled the place of proclamation; they have shut down the place of our sacred work; and they have left us with an empty stage, a Jumbo Tron, an ugly monitor at my feet, and a hand-held mike. Throw the mike on the floor and say, "Peace out!" That's your benediction? I don't think so!

Preaching matters. We do not need to replace our prophets with "life coaches," or be satisfied to leave Prayer Meeting in the hands of "inspirational speakers." In the words of William Augustus Jones, the culture always wants puppets but God requires prophets. We have come dangerously close to that time when it appears even our best seminaries are creating "pulpiteers" rather than preacher/prophets of the Most High God.

This is no time for ambivalence or malaise. Ours is a serious task and so it must be dealt with seriously. To view the shifting winds of the world, one must inevitably come to ask, "what in the world is the church *doing*?" and, quite obviously, of those who are called to the preaching task, "what in the world are we *saying*?"

With quivering pen in hand, I write these words on behalf of serious preaching. I seek to inspire serious students, who are ready to respond to God's call on their lives. Students who are ready to respond for serious study, who are serious about the call of God on their lives, with serious study and serious preaching that will prompt others to declare the unadulterated Gospel of Jesus Christ. I seek to inspire serious preachers willing to take on the blood-stained banner of Jesus Christ, to hold it high and let the world know that there is no salvation without the shedding of blood, and to remind them that *"The Blood Still Works!"*

Hear the urgency in these words of mine. This urgent appeal is for someone in this generation who will stand flat-footed, unashamed, and unapologetic and will speak the truths of God to a generation that is willing to believe anything, a generation that has grown up on the pabulum of apostasy and the spoiled milk of prosperity religion. It matters. Preaching Matters!

Our task as preachers of the Gospel is to take old, tired and hard to pronounce words, scattered words, complex words with complicated origins, and usher them into the presence of *The Word*, until old truths and an old Gospel become strangely new. You must take this word, set it in motion, and set it on the fire of the Holy Spirit until those who sit before it shall themselves be animated, inflamed and impassioned by the dance of that redemptive Gospel. Above all, do not fear the fire that is "shut up in your bones!" Preach!

. 2 .

The Process of Preaching

"How shall they preach?" That was the question the Apostle Paul shared with the Roman Christians who had come, Sabbath by Sabbath, to hear his testimony of faith. It was a question loaded with frightening implications and knotty conundrums. Paul had already made much of the fact that this would be something new for him—preaching in the Imperial City, the seat of the Caesars. And while he struggled to introduce himself to Jews and Gentiles, to Greeks and barbarians alike, Paul found it necessary to call out the various titles by which he was known: "Paul, a servant of Jesus Christ, called to be an apostle, separated unto the Gospel of God." (Rom. 1:1)

After only a few short verses, Paul sort of trips over his personal history and runs squarely into a reminder of that debt he owes to so many. Of them he says, "I *am debtor both to the Greeks and to the Barbarians; both to the wise and the unwise."* (Romans 1:14) In a sense, Paul knows he is living in the "Red." Yet it is precisely because of his debt and because of the investment so many have made in him, that he now stands to declare, "I'm ready!" I have been all over the known world, establishing churches and visiting with the faithful at their supper-boards. I have preached in churches big and small. I have tried to communicate with those churches in order that they "might be established." My passport is stamped with many ports of call; my sandals are soiled with the dust of many roads. That is why, after all of that, Paul could now say, "I'm ready." *"As much as in me is, I am ready to preach the gospel to you that are at Rome also."* (Rom. 1:15)

I think it is fair to say that God took the time to get Paul ready to preach. Paul had to go through a preparatory process. If Paul was to be used by God, God could not afford for Paul to be a "one-sermon-wonder!" God had to work with him.

Ask me how God makes a preacher and I will tell you, it is a process. Ups and downs, victories and defeats, trials and errors to be sure, but it is a process. In fact, Paul didn't get straight until he fell from his horse somewhere on the Damascus Road and bumped his head. So stunned and groggy was he from his fall that he had to be taken by the hand to Damascus, there to recuperate on a street called "Straight." It is a process. And you must not forget that Saul was hard to fit in preacher clothes. Acts 8 says quite clearly that *"he made havoc of the church, entering into every house, and haling men and women committed them to prison."* (Acts 8:3)

Yet now this Paul (the preacher formerly known as Saul), this persecutor turned preacher, this intellectually sophisticated and spiritually consecrated peripatetic disciple of Christ, declares himself to be a spokesman for the Eternal and pronounces that he is ready to preach. Think of it: Paul is a prisoner, bound hand and foot, deeply buried in solitary confinement and still he says that he is ready to preach. In a moment's time his head, and the heads of other road weary Christians like him, will roll in the grainy sawdust of the Roman Coliseum. Ready to preach? Indeed!

That's how God makes it happen! Here is the point of it all: before God releases you to prepare a *sermon*, God must first take the time to prepare *you!*

- God had to get Abraham and Sarah out of the Ur of the Chaldees to prepare them for a land He would show.
- God had to get Moses out of Goshen and let him stand amid burning bushes on Sinai for a while. God was just getting him ready.
- God had to rush Jeremiah down to the Potter's House, to the ghetto on the outskirts of the city in order to teach him that Israel and Jeremiah were both in His hands. That, however, was not enough. God had to reach into Jeremiah's cistern, lift him up and out,

simply to get him ready to preach and to prophesy.

If God had to work with these persons, how long will God have to work with you until you may be called a "Preacher!"?

To be sure, the ones that God chooses are not the ones I would choose. I'm still mystified as to why God would choose a Noah, the drunkard, or David, the philanderer, or Rahab the proprietor of the local brothel in Jericho, or Jeremiah, the crybaby. Surely God could have a better "bench" than these people. It seems to me a thing most strange that Jesus would tap the shoulder of that stutterer named Peter, or those radical firebrand brothers known as "Sons of Thunder," or Mary Magdalene about whom there remains much debate. More to the point, God's judgment really became questionable the day He chose me. And then God chose you!

So, then, we begin with the understanding that we do not preach because we are qualified, or because of our academic record, or because of our political associations. Understand me clearly: if you even *think* that God is calling you to preach, whatever you do, *don't run on your record! Don't rely on your resume!*

We preach in spite of ourselves. We preach in spite of the ambivalence of our faith. We preach in spite of our personal, tortured, sin-stained histories. Yet, God will not permit the record of our individual history to interfere with the future destiny of the people of God.

It was Ananias who described a blind Paul as a *"chosen vessel."* That's the only title we deserve, the only title we need: *Chosen vessel!* Jesus clarifies the matter: *"You have not chosen me; I have chosen you, and ordained you, that you should go and bring forth fruit. . . !"* (John 15:16a.) That is the reason why we preach. That is the warrant for our witness. That is the prerogative and the imperative for our preaching. We didn't qualify but He chose us anyhow! How awesome is that?!

Baking the Cake

I have two illustrations which may serve to help you understand what I mean by the process for preaching. This is the first.

From time to time I like to cook. Not often, mind you, only from time to time. I have special dishes that I like to prepare; they are always popular because my cooking gives my wife of fifty-three years a much-needed break. Recently I decided to try my hand at baking a cake. I consulted a cookbook and determined just what I would need in order to make this project a success. I turned the oven on to pre-heat at 325 degrees. I was determined to bake my pound cake no matter what. Of course I knew that failure and ridicule were just around the corner. So, I pulled out the flour, and the butter, and the vanilla extract, the eggs, the salt, and all the other things required for an astounding presentation at the close of dinner.

I lined up the ingredients across the kitchen counter in the order that they were called for in the recipe. This was easy. Who said baking a cake would be difficult? After all, I had a plan. I had never done it before but I had a plan.

As I look back upon the cooking process, I learned several lessons for preaching. Let's review a few of them:

- **Before one begins, it is important to read the recipe.** The recipe is the acknowledgement by the reader that he or she is not the first to bake a cake. Reading the recipe may reveal some secret ingredient that can spell the difference between a good cake and an outstanding culinary delight. There is value in reviewing the experience and expertise of those who have gone before. In other words, preacher, you don't know it all. It is possible for you to learn old recipes and new. There are lessons you can learn from others that just might strengthen your outcome. In my office on the credenza lay an old, old Bible, given by my mother to my father eighty years ago. The Book is called the Bible. In point of fact, however, it's a book filled with recipes, recipes for the living of our lives.

The first lesson, then, is clear: It is important to read the recipe. The "recipe" is a *"lamp unto (your) feet, and a light unto (your) path."* Read the "recipe." *"Man doth not live by bread only, but by every word that proceedeth out of the mouth of the Lord doth man live."* There is available to you a Bread of Heaven; there is a promise that He will feed you until you want no more. First, however, you must read the recipe!

- **Having the ingredients lined neatly in a row has no value**; sooner or later you must mix it up. Whether baking or preaching you must mix it up. You will not have a cake if you do not break some eggs and spill some flavor. Some shells must be broken. Things have to be stirred up; a wooden spoon is best. Don't give up, the batter gets thick. Where there is no stirring there will be no cake. Mix it up. There will be times when those who listen to you preach will not accept what they hear. So, you might as well mix it up. There will arise those who will reject every word you say. Remember, as my father would say, "you're not in management, you're in sales!" Have no fear. Say what you believe God has called you to say. *"For God hath not given us a spirit of fear, but of power and of love, and a sound mind."* Your recipe requires that you mix it up! Paul sent word to Timothy: "Stir up the gift of God that is in you through the laying on of hands."

- **(A private word intended for the Preacher/Baker).** In my experience, there have been times when I had everything and everyone lined up, in order, and ready to go. But the cake didn't rise. Despite my training, my preparation, my reading, my degrees and all the rest, things didn't work, the yeast failed, and the cake did not rise. Start over; don't quit. Sermon didn't work? Baking Powder didn't bake? Cake flopped in the pan? Cake didn't rise? Not to worry! In the words of Tony Campolo, **"It's Friday but Sunday's Coming!"** You will have another chance. Every failure is an opportunity to succeed. Rev. Willie Jolly says it this way. *"Every setback is a setup for a comeback."* The same God that fed the children of Israel with something called "Manna," surely that same God can handle you and your pound cake. Finally,

- **Don't leave anything out.** I have learned, in my brief cooking excursions, the importance of including all of the ingredients. Salt is a great example. While you don't want to use excessive salt, to leave the salt out of your cake entirely will insure that you have the best cornbread in town. Every recipe has been thought through by the author of the cookbook. Don't leave anything out.

Preach the "Whole Counsel of God." Preach the New Testament. Preach the Old Testament. After all, in the words of Dr. James Alvin Sanders, *"the Old Testament is as biblical as the New!"* Preach the prophets; preach the Epistles. Preach the Commandments as well as the Beatitudes. Preach sin but don't forget to preach grace.

This does not mean that our sermons must be lengthy *(after all, sermons to be immortal need not be eternal!)* but that over the expanse of one's ministry, we must leave nothing out; we must be thorough; we must fully participate in the process. Paul exhorted Timothy with this word:

> *"Reprove, rebuke, exhort with all long-suffering and doctrine. For the time will come when they will not endure sound doctrine.... and shall turn away their ears from the truth, and shall be turned unto fables. But watch thou in all things, endure afflictions, do the work of an evangelist, make full proof of thy ministry."*
> (II TIM. 4:2-4)

- **Don't forget the icing.** The icing makes the cake glorious. It is that last bit of sweetness that will linger on the tongue long after the cake is gone. The icing is not the cake, make no mistake, but it adds that something extra, something special to what may have been a dry and tasteless disaster. Many a sermon has come to an inglorious end for failure to put any icing on top. I am not suggesting that our sermon/cake be altered by some vain attempt to "sugarcoat" the Gospel or to make the sermon more acceptable to sinful palates.

I am suggesting, however, that Henry Wadsworth Longfellow, in his "Psalm of Life" reminds us that *"life is real! Life is earnest."* But whatever we are baking in the pulpit of our lives we cannot alter the reality we face but we can assist the reader or the hearer to accept life as it is with uncommon determination, grace, and faith.

This is the truth of these lessons: there are those who are, like a cake to be baked, on their way to an oven of oppressive heat and unparalleled pain. We know that, in the end, when the cake rises, they will be better off and in a better place. However, on some Sunday morning, if I can put the icing on top of someone's tortured life, if I can put some chocolate icing on top and let it spill over into the cracks and crevices for someone who is disturbed, depressed, distracted, and nearly destroyed by the exigencies of this life, and let them close their eyes and lick their fingers and click their heels because it tastes so good, I will then know that I have given them "strength for today and hope for tomorrow." I will know that I have at last preached the Gospel—the Good News of Jesus Christ.

By the way, what happened to the cake? Well, modesty makes me say that while it wasn't my best offering, still the cake didn't survive 24 hours on the kitchen counter. It appears that everyone is yet alive.

Pillars for Preaching

This is the second illustration. The ancient world, in Egypt, in the world of the Persians and certainly in Rome and in Greece, the landscape was punctuated with the presence of massive columns or pillars as a focal part of their architecture. Simply as a matter of interest the Greeks developed the classical orders of architecture, which are most easily distinguished by the form of the column and its various elements. Examples of their Doric, Ionic, and Corinthian orders were expanded by the Romans to include Tuscan and Composite orders. The purpose of the column or pillar, however, was a structural process that caused the weight of the structure above to be transmitted by compression to the weight of the structural elements below. Similar columns may be seen adorning many of the government buildings in our Nation's Capital. Also in the Botanical Gardens one will find Corinthian Columns just on the eastern edge of Washington, D.C.

Perhaps by purposeful introspection we may be able to see the pillars that will support as well as inform the preacher with the production of the weekly sermon that will consume so much of the preacher's life.

Let's be candid. The pastoral/preaching weight is heavy, demanding, and incessant. Compressed by demands of ministry and the needs of the people, and the preacher's natural hunger for a sense of "normalcy" in life, as well as a thirst for a spiritual life that is centered, grounded, and authentic, the stress of the preacher can be overwhelming. That's why I wanted to write this little book. So many pastors/preachers do not have *"pillars of support"* at their command.

Remember that pillars have a specific purpose; they are not there for their beauty nor for architectural embellishment alone. A pillar provides strength and support. A pillar can support the interior walls or ceiling. A pillar stays "engaged" to keep the wall supported. The pillar is there so that as the weight gets heavy the pillar helps to bear the burden. There are, then, seven pillars every preacher ought to have.

THE FIRST PILLAR: THE PREACHER'S PRAYER

Into every life some prayer must come. Often, so busy and involved, the preacher neglects his own need for that spiritual connection that only he can seek and only God can provide. There are others who will pray for the preacher, but the preacher must pray for him/her self. Sooner or later, however, the preacher will come to recognize the spiritual deficiency and to learn how to pray when no one is looking and no one can hear. He/she must learn to pray with our ancestors, *"Father I stretch my hands to Thee, no other help I know,"* and, in response, to give God *Total Praise!* It is in that "no other help" moment of time that the preacher/prophet will come to know the warm embrace of the Saviour.

Prayer is the pillar but the discipline of prayer is the foundation stone upon which the pillar rests. Prayer is the pillar that props up the preacher and strengthens the preacher to preach with power the preacher did not know was available; quite literally prayer shapes, surrounds, and lifts the preacher for the preaching moment. The preacher/pastor may be so caught up in praying for others, at one hospital or another, that often he neglects his own salvation and discounts the disappearing relationship with the God of His salvation. The Apostle Paul said it this way: *"I keep under my body, and bring it unto subjection: lest that by any means, when I have preached to others, I myself should be a castaway."* (I Cor: 9:27)

THE SECOND PILLAR: CONVERSION AND CONVICTION
I should not have to ask these questions: Are you converted? Are you saved? Have you been born again? Have you been baptized down in Jordan's chilly stream? Do you know God in the pardoning of your sins? Have you been washed in the precious blood of the Lamb? If you died tonight do you know where you're going?

These are not casual or unimportant questions. (If you are having a doctrinal issue right now, please excuse me but I am a regularly ordained, Baptist preacher and I can't help myself!) *"With the heart man belie-*

veth and with the mouth confession is made unto salvation." (Rom. 10:10)

Now then, if you have been converted and born again, you have warrant to permit you to confess your "call" to the Preaching ministry. Be careful, however, of that four-letter word: "Call." Do not *think* of preaching unless and until there is a sure and certain life connection between you and the Eternal. This *Calling God* does not "call" all in just the same way, in just the same place, or in the same time. He may come while you, like Samuel, are fast asleep. And God will call you by your name and your only response may be, "Speak Lord, thy servant heareth." That's when He teaches you to say, "I hear you! I hear you!" But if you haven't heard Him, roll over and go back to sleep.

Twin Pillars! One is called conversion and the other is conviction. Conviction says, 'I have decided to follow Jesus, no turning back, no turning back. Conviction says, "For me to live is Christ; to die is gain." Conviction says, "As for me and my house, we will serve the Lord." Conviction says, in the words of our ancestors, "Ain't gonna let nobody turn me around." Conversion and conviction—you need them both.

Remember, however, that the "Call" of God requires a binary line. Be careful that you are not listening to so many voices that when God does call all God hears is: **"I'm sorry but the party you are calling is not accepting calls now and the mailbox is full. Good-bye."**

The "call" requires two things—an open ear, willing to hear and to be receptive to the voice of God and an open heart, broken and contrite, humbled yet expectant, ready to be used in God's service. Keep the prayer line open; keep the relationship full and free. By the way, you may return the call. I love to hear the authentic church ring out the old song: "Jesus is on the main line; tell Him what you want!"

THE THIRD PILLAR: STANDING ON BIBLE GROUNDS OR WEDDED TO THE WORD

Let me say it quite plainly and without fear of successful contradiction. Any preaching that is not Bible-based and grounded is not a sermon. It may be a speech. It may be a lecture; it may be an academic paper; it may be an essay or a blog post but it is certainly not a sermon.

That, however, is not why you must remain wedded to the Word. You must do so because the Word will inform you of how God has worked with your interior being to such an extent it has been grafted into your body and scientists call it your DNA. Accordingly, your DNA certifies your identity. It tells who you are and from where you have come. It explains the connections with previous generations and the connections you will have with generations yet to come.

There are questions you should be asking: What is my spiritual DNA? What is it about me that senses a deep connection with what the Bible teaches? What do the Scriptures say to my life? What is it about this book that so transparently speaks to me? After all, if the Word has not spoken to you, how will you convince others that the Word will speak to them? There is a rich devotional and meditative life available to you within the Word; it is a deep spiritual well from which to draw and by which, week by week, preachers have been renewed and sermons are born.

If I were you I would hang around the Word. I would meet some great people there: Abraham, Isaac, and Jacob. Sarah, Rebekah, and Leah and Rachael. I'd meet Samson and Delilah, David and Bathsheba, Solomon, Saul and Jonathan. Then I'd sure walk down Jeremiah's avenue and ask him, "What's up?" I would then slip over to Isaiah's house and sit on the back porch and rock for a spell.

And then I'd meet Matthew, Mark, Luke, and John. I'd meet Mary and Martha and Lazarus and the whole gang down at Bethany Cemetery. I'd meet the man at Bethesda Pool, those ten lepers, and the woman with an issue of blood. And, oh yes, I would see Jesus for myself. Just hang around the Bible; I dare you.

The Bible has God for its author and salvation as its end. "The grass withereth, the flower fadeth, but the Word of our God shall stand forever." (Isa. 40:8) Preach the Word!

The Book of Hebrews reminds us that "Through faith we understand that the worlds were framed by the Word of God so that the things which are seen were not made of things which do appear." (Heb. 11:3) Preach the Word!

Young Preacher! Old Preacher! Paul gave this advice to Timothy: *"Preach the Word: be instant in season, out of season: reprove, rebuke, exhort with all long-suffering and doctrine. For the time will come when they will not endure sound doctrine: but after their own lusts shall they heap to themselves teachers, having itching ears."* (II Tim. 4:2-3)

THE FOURTH PILLAR: SELF-MASTERY—
FAMILY FIRST

The young preacher (as well as the old) must always remember that the reason he or she is a preacher in the first place is because they have a family that lets him or her do so. This pillar is a simple one. The family is the one group of people you can count on. There are all kinds of people who will fill your head with nonsense—"Reverend, you certainly were awesome today. Reverend, your words just spoke to my spirit; you just set my soul on fire."

You can believe that if you want to but believe this: you've got to go home. Nobody else will be there to rub your back that hurts because you stood too long. Nobody else will know the real story of how high your mountains or how low your valleys. Do not be deceived.

The imposters called "popularity," and "success," intellectual gifts, your picture in the paper, good looks, and financial prowess will vanish with the morning dew. Go to the soccer game. Coach the basketball team. Take time to help with homework. Take care of your family—love them, honor them, protect them, provide for them, and then remember that they are still there, waiting for you to come home.

There is a second priority attached to this pillar which is a necessary corollary of the first: **Self-Mastery**. Modestly defined it means, "contain yourself." Better yet, it is called "Self-Control." Be twice cautious. As my brother, William, is fond of saying, "If the crowd is going east, make it your business to go west." Believe half of what you see and none of what you hear. The confidence you build in your congregation will be in direct proportion to your ability to contain yourself. Contain your ego. Contain your tongue.

Let me tell you of Frederick W. Robertson, a nineteenth century preacher named Bishop in the Holy Trinity Church in Brighton, England. It was said of Bishop Robertson that, *"By of the measure of his restraint which he laid upon his own emotions he was able to stir the emotion of others. Perhaps nothing else so quite subdues a public audience as the spectacle in a speaker of supreme self-command. Nothing else so gives him a title to command others as a wise self-command."* Not only that, *"He built his pulpit into an altar and bound himself to and consumed himself on it, God sanctifying the gift. He burned all of himself on the altar at the center of his ministry."*

THE FIFTH PILLAR: ELIJAH'S MANTLE
—OR, CAN GOD TRUST YOU?

There are persons, men and women, devout of faith, faithful proclaimers of the Gospel that you and I will never meet until we gather somewhere around the throne of God. Fortunately for us their thoughts, motives, emotions, and their words remain; we are beneficiaries of that grace.

I suggest to you, much in the manner of Elisha, that you find and attach yourself to an Elijah from whom you can gain much insight and meaningful direction for your days and for your ministry. Find some pillar of grace that will support you and sustain you in every hour of weakness and imperfection. You will, of course, remember that preachers are not perfect, nor should they be. You and I should be dismissed from their coterie if they were. Indeed, we all have struggles, compulsions, and passions that greet us every day with the morning sun. By some means or other we have all been crippled by this thing called humanity. We all have weakness in some area of our lives. We all have our own "thorn in the flesh" with which to contend. There is always some "prick" in life that causes us to bleed.

And so, we have "issues," every one of us. Issues that make us who we are. We have issues that are not to be denied. Yet, if you find an old Prophet around and let him tell his story, no doubt you will find that the issues they reveal are sum and substance of the reason for the greatness they have attained. 'Tis strange, but true but sometime God removes things from us (our health, our employment, a loved one, a church, a relationship) to get us to see where he wants us to be and to use us for His glory and His alone. Maybe that's what Job really meant: "The Lord giveth and the Lord taketh away!" It is in the "taking away" process that God provides the room for gifts and graces far beyond our imagination.

CONSIDER THESE PREACHERS AS MODELS:
Known as the Prince of Preachers, **Charles Haddon Spurgeon** was a British "Particular" Preacher who remains highly influential to this day. *Christianity Today* reports him to have said, "I am perhaps vulgar, but it is not intentional, save that I must and will make people listen." Underneath, however, is the real story. Spurgeon suffered greatly with rheumatism and gout that greatly affected his life.

Wyatt T. Walker, Pastor of Harlem's Canaan Baptist Church, is former Chief of Staff to Martin Luther King. It has been said that in his day he preached with the lyrical quality of biblical prophets; and yet he speaks in an authentic voice. They called him Harlem's Renaissance Man. As author, cultural historian, and theologian, Dr. Walker has written and published more than twenty books. Many of those books he has written by computer using only one finger as a consequence of his numerous strokes of which he wrote in a volume titled, *My Stroke of Grace*.

Dr. Renita Weems was celebrated by *Ebony Magazine* as one of America's greatest preachers and is the first

African American woman to earn a PhD as a Hebrew Bible scholar. While she was celebrated for her accomplishments she wrestled with her own faith—due to experiencing the absence of God's voice for a protracted period of time. Ultimately, her faith was renewed and reinforced and she shares with us this assessment: "Our deepest, most painful wounds not only leave us with scars that we bear forever, but also, if we make our peace with them, leave us wiser, stronger, more sensitive than we otherwise would have been had we not been afflicted with them."[14]

While I'm on my way, let me point you to **Charles Edward Booth**, Senior Pastor of the Mount Olivet Baptist Church in Columbus, Ohio. As I recall it some years ago in 1996 I was invited to attend the Hampton University Ministers' Conference to lecture to that amazing gathering, literally thousands upon thousands of learned African American preachers, pastors, and scholars.

I was to lecture in Ogdon Hall but Dr. Booth was to precede me in speaking. As I approached the Hall, I recognized persons stretched out on the grounds, many furiously fighting brows of perspiration, waving their funeral home fans, hoping desperately to chase the heat away. What I soon discovered was this: because of the preaching of the hour (not the outside temperature!) but the temperature of the Holy Spirit

---

14   Weems, Renita J. , "Listening for God: A Minister's Journey Through Silence and Doubt," Touchstone/Simon Schuster, New York, NY. , p. 22.

had so overwhelmed the house. Preachers will say, "there were not enough living to bury the dead." It was an awesome scene. In his sermon, however, Charles Booth revealed what many did not know—he is totally blind in his left eye. He spoke of his sainted mother and how she had counseled him never to think of himself as in any way crippled or handicapped, or different in any way but to remember that by God's grace he could stand and do what others could do in spite of whatever obstacle he happened to face. The lesson: whatever your impediment, you can overcome it. Yes, you can!! The time-honored preacher's wisdom on this point is, of course, never stand in another preacher's fire.

By the way, I never gave that lecture.

Gardner Calvin Taylor, of the Concord Church of Christ in Brooklyn, New York, was hailed by *Time Magazine* as "the greatest preacher in the English-speaking world," while *Christian Century* described him as "the greatest preacher living, dead or unborn." And yet, this great preacher walked with a limp and appeared unable to stand erect. Somehow the winds of time had robbed him of life unhindered; you hardly noticed and he never discussed it. But he left this word for aspiring preachers: *"Preparation brings you to your pulpit but prayer brings the Holy Spirit there. The real key of a successful ministry is a broken heart. God can only fill the place that has been emptied of the joys of this life."*

I still hear the name of **Vashti Murphy McKenzie**. A powerful preacher, a scholar, a woman of wisdom and grace. Few understand the pressure under which she waged a valiant struggle to become the first female Bishop elected to that office in the 213-year history of the African Methodist Episcopal Church. In every sense of the word, her handicap and her sin was her gender. Still she has become one of America's leading African American clergy women. She speaks of her struggle in this way:

> The greatest frustration is seeing
> those whose hand you
> Have held and helped to fight
> for a better community
> And church turn against you.
> They go through the door
> First and then close it in your face.
> It is not because you are
> Incompetent, untrained, unskilled.
> Unprepared, or stupid:
> It is not because you haven't been called of God,
> It is because you are female.
>
> Only the committed and continual strength
> of both genders,
> Serving with each other and not pitted
> against each other,
> Will propel us toward a biblical egalitarianism.
> The men
> Will not make it without the women.
> The women will
> Not make it without the men.

BUT IT WILL ALWAYS BE:
NOT WITHOUT A STRUGGLE!

It's called personal integrity. It's called knowing our limits and our liabilities. It's called standing before the world with honor, chastened by our own faults yet able to share with others empowered by forgiveness and grace. It's called accepting life's handicaps as the gift of God's grace and not as God's sentence of judgement. It's called accepting the wise counsel and example of those who have gone before you and have been where you are headed.

Follow the example these persons represent. They are not to be revered as paragons of virtue but as examples of frail servants who endured the pain and the shame all the while holding up the blood-stained banner of our Christ.

To understand the Art of Preaching and the preachers who have walked in that path is not only to appreciate their history but to understand your coming place in that long line of history as well. The library is filled with the storied record of preachers, male and female, who have achieved both because of and in spite of great odds, great obstacles, and great challenges. Those challenges did not stop them; they made them strong, uncovering a depth of strength even they may not have known they had.

One name remains which must never be omitted. Among the advantages of being a "PK", (Preacher's Kid) was the number of traveling preachers who stopped in our home for a night's lodging. I remember so many of them by name:

> Cornel Talley Central / Pittsburgh
> James Casey Ebenezer / Pittsburgh
> Sandy Ray Cornerstone / Brooklyn
> Thomas Kilgore Second / Los Angeles
> Gardner Taylor Concord / Brooklyn

And my personal favorite, Wendell T. Liggins, Zion / Denver who took time out from preparing to preach to teach me how to shine my shoes.

These and so many others came and took their place at Eleanor Hicks' dining room table. I found my seat in the corner near the window and there I listened as those preaching giants told of their journey in ministry. Their stories came to life by their glib tongues and of course, the telling of "preacher jokes" far into the night. The interaction among the preachers was, for me, real and life changing—more than I could have possibly known.

On the night of September 19, 1962, the night of my sister, Sandra's wedding, a new chair was brought to the Saturday night table. The preacher's called him by his nickname—Mike—but the rest of the world called him Martin Luther King, Jr. Clearly Martin King was the role model, the exemplar, the consummate standard of what it meant to be both preacher and prophet.

If he was a preacher, one has only to see him in his role as a theological student, or to see him as pastor, first in Alabama and at last in Georgia.

If he was a prophet, one has only to hear of his skillful handling of the scriptures or listen to the eloquence of his speech or the resonate cadence of his words.

On the other hand ...

If prophet, one had only to follow in his footsteps to see him come face to face with the ugliness of racism and speak to bigotry without fear.

If prophet, one only had to walk with him down the back roads of hatred, or listen as his words brought the nation to a halt and cause her to abandon her headlong descent toward violence and the catastrophe of national godlessness.

I need not say more; no doubt you can fill in the blanks and tell this story better than I. I do believe, however, that Martin King was both preacher and prophet.

This is what I think we need to remember. We must never forget that Martin King was flesh and blood, a preacher, yes; but no paragon of virtue.

A prophet, yes; but not without sin or shortcoming.

A prophet, yes; yet he was a man whose chest was opened by a would-be assassin's dagger.

A prophet, yes; yet it was a man who was besieged by those who disagreed violently with his stand against the War in Vietnam.

A prophet, yes; and yet it was a man who left his wife and children alone at home while he made his way to Memphis, there to speak on behalf of garbage workers in that city only to be carried to his untimely grave by a mule drawn flatbed.

A prophet, yes; yet that is what propelled him to stand in the shadow of Abraham Lincoln and declare before the world, "I Have a Dream!"

The question is, where are you on that continuum? Are you preacher or prophet? Are you neither or are you both? The question is whether God can trust you to do it His way. Will you seek out your Elijah? Will you make yourself available to be taught, to receive instruction, to be humble before the Prophet God has sent to instruct you? Can God trust you to contain yourself before the bright lights of the Mega-Church and be content to wait for the Chariot of Angels God is sure to send for your eternal escort? It's something to think about.

Ah, yes. When you come to consider the finality of life, remember these words of Dr. Gardner Calvin Taylor, honored as the Poet Laureate of Preachers the world over: *"Above all, there is in each of us a dis-ease, a sense of un-fulfillment of some high destiny unmet, of some lofty vow, broken and shattered. We are sinners! We long for some word of forgiveness which will make us whole. We sense we have a homeland but we are exiles. We perceive that we are of royal lineage, but our lives are being spent cheaply and shabbily and our purposes and ends far too narrow and parochial. We would be restored to our true estate."*[15] This is the predicament we face individually; it is the reason that we must preach to others but most especially must we preach to ourselves.

THE SIXTH PILLAR: GUARD YOUR GIFT

No one may have told you. No one may have shared the news. Jesus is the gift of God to the world but you, dear reader, are a gift to the body of Christ. What you shall do and what you shall become is not in our minds to know nor in our hands to achieve. What we do know is that you are the gift and God is the giver.

The question for now is "what will you do with your gift?" You are reading this book perhaps because somewhere in your mind is the irrepressible notion that God is calling you to ministry. You are sure you have something to offer but you are not quite sure just what it is. You know that your gift is to be used but you don't know what to do with the angst, the fear and the trepidation that calling occasions.

Come now and remember the words which Paul sent to Timothy, his son in the Gospel. The salutation of his letter is typically Pauline but he moves rather swiftly to matters personal in the body of his letter. Paul wants to remind Timothy how he had shared with his fore-parents and sought to assure him that his prayers for Timothy continued "without ceasing."

---

15   Taylor, Gardner, "How Shall They Preach?" Lyman Beecher Lectures. Progressive Baptist Publishing House, Elgin, IL, 1977.

Looking forward to visiting with Timothy, Paul was nearly brought to tears. That's when memory really took over. When Paul began to think of Timothy's faith and how it had been passed along through the bloodlines of the generations, a faith first detected in Timothy's grandmother, Lois, and then demonstrated in his mother, Eunice; there was no way the gifts of grace and faith Paul had seen in those two admirable women were not also present in Timothy. That's why Paul fairly shouted: *"Stir up the gift of God which is in thee by the putting on of my hands."* Says Paul, "Listen, I licensed you, I ordained you, I consecrated you, I anointed you, I know you have something in you. Now, stir up the gift."

It is important now to remind the reader that Timothy Keller is spot on when he reminds us all that "the difference between good preaching and great preaching lies mainly in the work of the Holy Spirit in the heart of the listener as well as the preacher... I cannot give you a formula for great preaching—and no one can—because that secret lies in the depths of God's wise plans and the power of God's Spirit. I'm talking about what many have referred to as "unction" or "anointing."[16]

That is why I feel a certain unction even in this moment to share a word with an unknown reader and assure them that this word is directed to them. Be open to the action of the Holy Spirit; feel the movement of wind and fire in yourself even as it becomes manifest

---

16 Keller, Timothy. Ibid. , p. 11.

in those you serve. Stir up your gift. Stir up the gift until the stale and polluted waters of your being are moving and fit for life. Stir up the gift until the detritus litter of life is removed and you are able to be baptized in refreshing springs.

But do not simply stir it up. You must also guard your gift. Protect your gift. Never let your gift be used for vainglory. Never let your gift be used by enemies who will come against you with weapons to destroy you. Guard your gift from unholy hands. Do not be shy to tell them, "Touch not mine anointed, and do my prophets no harm..." (Ps. 105:15) Let no man, let no woman, make vile that which is sacred before God.

THE SEVENTH PILLAR: TRUST HIM

The seventh and final pillar needs no exposition. It means what it says: Trust Him. When in doubt, trust Him. When tossed about, trust Him. When the path is unclear, trust Him. When roadblocks appear in your path, trust Him. His promises are sure, his presence is permanent, his love is limitless and His grace is sufficient for everything you may need. Just now, you are not certain that you have been "called." So stand still until His will is clear and, in the meantime, trust Him.

Only God knows with surety the kind of preacher you are destined to become. Your destiny is in God's hands and not in your own. Your destiny is sealed within the boundaries of your personality. To understand the metes and measures of your personality will be the challenge of your life. Dr. Taylor expresses this notion this way:

> *The opportunity and privilege of the preacher is to find out his or her dominant response that their personality makes to the gospel. Of course, the text will dictate how that through line is applied, but you will discover it and God deliver you from a deadening, monotony, Johnny-One-Note preaching. You will discover it according to your personality that a particular aspect of the gospel will almost invariably come out in anything that you preach.*
> *It is authentic, it is your authority, it is the authenticity of your own personality.* [17]

You are not certain what to do? You are not certain what to say? You have questions for which you have no answers? Again, I say, *"stand still until His will is clear."*

Or you are certain, perhaps, that God has called you into active ministry but you are scared to death. Here's my advice: Trust Him and He will lead you to life.

> *The service of Jesus true pleasure affords,*
> *In Him there is joy without an alloy.*
> *'Tis heaven to trust Him and rest on His words;*
> *It pays to serve Jesus each day.*
> *Tho' sometimes the shadow may hang o'er the way,*
> *And sorrows may come to beckon us home,*
> *Our precious Redeemer each toil will repay,*
> *It pays to serve Jesus each day.*
> *It pays to serve Jesus,*

---

[17] Thomas, Gerald Lamont, "African American Preaching: The Contribution of Dr. Gardner C. Taylor," Peter Lang Publishing, Inc., New York, p. 109. 14 Huston, Frank C. :library. timelesstruths. org/music.

It pays every day.
It pays every step of the way.
Tho' the pathway to glory
May sometime be drear,
You'll be happy each step of the way.[18]

---

18 Huston, Frank C., library. timelesstruths. org/music.

. 3 .

Part I: The Prophetic Pulpit

To Prophesy or Not?

> **Preach.** *Predicare,* to preach the gospel < L. to proclaim, declare in public ... 1. To speak in public on religious matters; give a sermon 2. To give moral or religious advice, esp. in a tiresome manner—vt. 1. To expound or proclaim by preaching 3. To advocate by or as by preaching; urge strongly or persistently 3. To deliver a sermon.
>
> **Preacher.** a person who preaches; esp. a clergyman.
>
> **Prophet.** < Gr. *Prophetes*, interpreter of a god's will (in LLX a Hebrew Prophet; in N. T. an inspired preacher) 1. A person who speaks for God or a god, or as though under divine guidance 2. A religious teacher or leader regarded as, or claiming to be divinely inspired 3. A spokesman for some cause, group movement. 4. A person who predicts (or foreshadows) future events in any way.
>
> WEBSTER'S NEW WORLD DICTIONARY
Second College edition 1986

> "Then answered Amos, and said to Amaziah. I was no prophet, neither was I a prophet's son; but I was an herdsman and a gatherer of sycamore fruit. And the Lord took me as I followed the flock, and the Lord said unto me, Go, prophesy unto my people Israel."
>
> (AMOS 7:14-15)

The similarities are many. The distinctions, however, are clear. It is important that we understand these definitions; for it is by these definitions that we come to know who we are, what we are to become, and how we are to serve.

Midway through the second decade of the twenty-first century, I fear something is missing from our religious enterprise. We who stand from time to time in vaulted cathedrals, we who stand in those halls where theologians gather, or who preach from elevated platforms designed for the oft times theatrical staging for our preaching, have come now to the uncomfortable realization that something is tragically wrong; something is missing from the church.

In this respect, Marvin McMickle, former pastor of the Antioch Church in Cleveland, Ohio, and now President of Colgate Rochester Divinity School in Rochester, New York has raised a pivotal question for our time. In his writing, Dr. McMickle raises the question: ***"Where have all the Prophets gone?"*** [19] The question and its implications are startling. Is it so that for all our preach-

---

[19] McMickle, Marvin. "Where Have All the Prophets Gone?" The Pilgrim Press, Cleveland, Ohio 2006.

ing, somehow the prophets have gone missing? What is even more startling, however, is the sub-title to his text: *"Reclaiming Prophetic Preaching in America."*

His question raises others:

If we must *reclaim* the prophetic then who took it from us? Or, if prophetic preaching were ever ours to claim or to keep then, tell me, how careless were we that it ever slipped through our hands?

If prophetic preaching must be reclaimed and if those who were once ordained and set apart as prophets have gone, what timid voices are these sub-prophetic imposters that speak so meekly now in the places where authentic prophets once boldly proclaimed Eternal truths?

How tragic is it that the voices of those who should be prophets have now been strangely stilled into silence, and those who should be garbed with the prophetic mantle are now afflicted by a laryngitis that renders the church mute and therefore spiritually ineffective?

With the crisis about and within the government of this land, how tragic is it that for selfish purposes there has not been heard one clear and clarion voice from the church or its prophetic ranks to speak forthrightly God's word for our times? It seems to me that the challenge we face is to clearly identify those who have earned the right to be called "Prophet" rather than to promote those who simply want to be prophet, or to elevate those who seek the title only to be available when the television cameras are rolling—when *CNN* wants to call our name.

How shall we wake up the feeble and the fearful who shun the robes and garments of the pulpit but who prefer to play it safe in order to avoid recriminations or be exposed by some public finger of blame or shame. The church then becomes a hiding place. I can hide in the church on Sunday but I won't be available on Monday. You will hear me well on a Sabbath morning but my voice will be mute when the conflict erupts on Monday. I will be available for Prayer Meeting but count me out for the Civic meeting.

Those who would be prophets must know that there is no religion without risk. This job requires not that you are a fortune teller but rather a "forth" teller—the prophet speaks forth and brings forth the Word of God. This comes alone from God, the fulfillment of which is in God's hands and God's alone.

Above all is the test of prophecy. The only way to know if a person is a prophet is whether or not the prophecy comes true. Long before we rise to preach our congregations are able to see behind the drawn curtains of stifling traditions and bogus anointments. They will know most assuredly that we have failed the prophetic test.

How one speaks, how one dresses, and how many platforms you ascend is not the standard of your success. Prophet, is your prophecy authentic, is it real, is it true? Over and over that refrain must be in your head: Is it true? People will come to hear you but before they leave and before the benediction, some soul on the third row will ask the question, "Is It True?"

This may be the problem within the theological community—no one wants to sign up to be a prophet. There is no one teaching it—no one seeking it—no one signing up for the latest seminary course on *How to be a Prophet 101*. Academic committees are not insistent on adding prophetic classes to the curriculum.

Here's the problem. In fact, there may be two. The first problem is how do prophets get to be prophets? Who established the prophetic criteria? Who determines the professional guidelines? In contemporary African American religious culture there seems to be a small gathering of persons who decide who is and who is not "worthy" of ancient ecclesiastical titles.

Prophets chosen in this manner are very often the same personalities who embody the paternalistic, misogynistic personalities that have for generations fostered inequities and discrimination against women, gender and other minorities within the African American church; the same women that for years have sustained the church by offerings, free labor, and innate leadership that has literally kept the Black Church alive. We may as well acknowledge that there is within the Black Church an "Old Guard," an "Old Boys Club" or some other instrument of repressive power designed to keep the status quo. The problem with self-appointment, of course, is that there is no one around with the power of disappointment.

In like manner, if it is true that there are those who are called prophet by some mysterious and ethereal group, there are significant numbers of persons who are not appointed by committee; rather, they are self-appointed. I have only this to say: Beware False Prophets. Their attractiveness to the camera lens is always short lived. I believe it was the Epistle of John that suggested that we "try or test the spirits to see if they be of God!"

Then again, too many prophets may have appeared within the African American Church because of an over-active ego, massaged by that evil devil called "Money." Many a prophet has been bought off and brought low by the instrument of an overflowing offering basket. In sum, never seek the pulpit; let the pulpit seek you.

Someone sound the alarm—our people are abandoning the church! Not Jesus, mind you, just the church. The church is abandoned because those who yet remain in her pews are people of intelligence and "street creds" who can see a scam before it materializes. Live streaming and social media may be all that is left because the world can see through our worship and confuse our worship with entertainment. I am aware of the advantages of modern technology and do not intend to be out of step. What concerns me, however, are twenty-first century Christians who turn to the computer for information, news, and entertainment but see no reason at all to respond to the summons to assemble together for praise. Many who have departed from the church are now members in good standing at Bedside Baptist or Pillow Presbyterian. Offerings sent in electronically at the touch of a button are a poor substitute for Malachi 3 and the promise of window blessings we won't be able to receive.

The sum of it all is that when you add the work of self-appointment to high position and lofty titles, added to mysterious committees that make determinations that no one can define or defy—when there are too many standing on the outside of leadership with their noses pressed against the window and they are kept from membership in the "Old Boys Club," and when so called "leading preachers" gather outside a millionaire's tower in search of a job or some political appointment, that is the reason people leave the church or know for themselves that the one they are listening to is not a prophet.

Those who seem to be the acknowledged prophets of this age do not seek to be unpopular. They prefer, rather, the bright lights, the informal "Praise Teams," cameo visits on TBN, live streaming TV, professional singing artists, and the comfortable seats of the mega-church. Those who seem to be the prophets of this age do not stand against the culture; they prefer not to speak to the issues of poverty and pain, the problems of helplessness and homelessness, the hungry and the heartbroken. They do not take the risk of speaking truth to power.

To tell the truth, no one wants to be a prophet. Maybe no one should ever want to be a prophet.

Prophets tend to be unpopular.

Prophets tend to have difficulty justifying their right to the title they claim.

Prophets tend to stand over against and counter to the culture.

Prophets are expected to speak without fear and with little regard for the prohibitions of the state.

Prophets tend to preach with a voice that is raised, an urgency that cannot be escaped and a fire that cannot be quenched.

And yet, somebody must stand to prophesy.

When the church remains silent on matters of the dismantling of Affordable Health Care or fails to address those issues that speak to fundamental humanity and compassion, where are the prophets?

When racism rears again its ugly head while the culture proclaims itself to be post-racism, where are the prophets?

When the new politics of the day permit the carrying of guns in the public square, when new leadership within government agencies promotes the permission for firearms in public schools, when public discourse is ever crude and never civil, when Congressmen are spat upon while passing in the streets, when the leadership of racist and supremacists groups have entrée into the inner-circles of the White House, to include groups such as neo-Nazis, fascists, and the KKK, when the President of these United States is unable to call evil and hate by its own name, and when the only party which seems to have struck a chord with the American conscience is something called "Alt-Right" and the church says not a word, tell me, where have all the prophets gone? Indeed!

Church, State, and Prophecy

With appropriate deference to the time-honored principal of the separation of church and state, the problem may be not that the pulpit has said too much but that the pulpit has said too little. What is the source of this iniquitous silence that seems to have overtaken the pulpits of the land?

Marvin McMickle unpacks for us the whole question of church and state. In a precise and piercing statement Dr. McMickle helps us to understand what that phrase does and does not mean since many are of the opinion that the principle is designed to prevent the church from speaking to or directly confronting the political establishment of the nation.

"If the fear of an established religion was the problem confronting the founders of this country, then the separation of church and state, and the guarantee of religious liberty, was the solution that they adopted to protect these rights for all citizens." McMickle goes on to remind us that "the actual words "separation of church and state" do not appear anywhere in the constitution."[20]

McMickle skillfully points to G. K. Chesterton who described the United States as *"a nation with the soul of a church,"* and goes on to say that "this is how the power of politics can and should work together, treating all people as if they matter. There is a place for people of religious faith, including clergy, in the political process, to make sure that politics works to care for the least of these and not just for the richest and wealthiest among us."[21]

Stephen L. Carter in his work titled *The Culture of Disbelief,* subtitled *How American Law and Politics Trivialize Religious Devotion,* makes McMickle's argument crystal clear: *"...the metaphorical separation of church and state originated in an effort to protect religion from the state and not the state from religion. The religion clauses of the First Amendment were crafted to permit maximum freedom to the religious...it does not mean, however, that people whose motivations are religious are banned from trying to influence government, nor that the government is banned from listening to them. Understanding this distinction is the key to preserving the necessary separation of church and state without resorting to a philosophical*

---

20 McMickle, Marvin A. , "Pulpit & Politics: Separation of Church and State in the Black Church," Judson Press: Valley Forge, Penna. , p. 20-21.
21 Ibid. p. 21

rhetoric that treats religion as an inferior way for citizens to come to public judgment."[22]

One should also note as Carter points out, the Free Exercise Clauses were designed to secure religious liberty, which Thomas Jefferson called *"the most inalienable and sacred of all human rights."*[23] The more one reads on the issue of church and state the more it becomes the apparent duty of those in high moral leadership positions to speak boldly to the body politic. William Augustus Jones, late Pastor of the Bethany Church in Brooklyn, summarizes the matter as only he could, **"Preachers no longer have to ask permission to be prophetic."**

In addition, Robert McAfee Brown challenges us to see political involvement as a "means of grace," and warns us that "we shirk our fundamental duty if we do not at least attempt to influence and even wield some power that affects the lives of many millions of our fellow citizens including members of our own congregations."[24]

Martin King rounds out this discussion in a statement encouraging the embrace of Christian ideals of equality, freedom, and justice as demanded by the Word of God.

---

22 Carter, Stephen L., "The Culture of Disbelief," BasicBooks, HarperCollins, 1993, p. 105f.
23 Ibid., p. 106
24 Ibid. p. 42

> *"It has been my conviction,"* said King, *"ever since reading Rauschenbusch that any religion which professes to be concerned about the souls of men and is not concerned with the social and economic conditions that scar the soul is a spiritually moribund religion only waiting to be buried. It has been well said: 'A religion that ends with the individual, ends."*[25]

Particularly, in relationship to the African American church experience, it is clear that the condition of slavery and servitude was the birthplace of activism and involvement in the political process which many would be loath to remember. That the church, and particularly the African American church, should remain silent and politically neutral, was the context of the controversy over Presidential Candidate Barack Obama and his involvement with the "radical" Pastor, Rev. Jeremiah Wright. Historically, Black preachers have been seen most often as empowered leaders who serve as a counterforce to the winds of oppression that were intended to keep Black people powerless and voiceless.[26] This is the "way," this is the "why" Black people must cry out again and again, **"Black Lives Matter."**

Is it relevant? **That is the question.** The whole conversation of the separation of church and state has to

---

[25] King, Martin Luther, Stride toward Freedom, Harper and Row Publishers, New York, NY. ,1964, p. 73.
[26] Ibid. p. 113

do with the church and its capacity as well as its readiness to use whatever resources may be available as we strive to extend the life of the church going forward. Clearly, as we candidly view the values and the interests of this generation, it is more than apparent that the church must change or suffer even greater loss of its constituency and, not inconsequentially, its reason for being will be void and of none effect.

Even more apparent is not that the church has lost its grip on this generation but what this generation has found to replace it. I take the position that with the candidacy of Barack Obama in 2008, he took some of the organizational structures and leadership principles found most often in the church and turned the world upside down. Wittingly or not, this experienced community organizer had his own brand of "church;" he called it a campaign. He turned the crowd into a choir and then taught them how to sing "Yes we can!" "We shall Overcome" had become too future oriented. On the other hand, "Yes we can" was affirmative, right now, and immediate. This was the word we needed to hear; this was the song we needed to sing at this particular moment of human history. This "preacher," unlicensed and unordained, nevertheless had captured the principle that before he could count on the vote of the people, the people needed to know they could count on him. His success was insured when the people discovered that there was something about this man. They heard his words but they could see through the words to his heart. Barack Obama knew that beyond the noisy political in-fighting and squabbling of those still seeking a voice that would be heard and a justice that could not be denied, there breathed the soul of a people who, when put to work constructively, would know no limits, no bounds.

The progeny of those who marched on Washington for freedom in 1963 now marched all over the land in search of the brass ring—the Presidency. Field hands and Sunday School teachers marched and waded in all over the South until they arrived at the Reflecting Pool of the Lincoln Memorial. Those same folk walked and campaigned for Mr. Obama but now they were joined by BA's, and MA's, and MBA's and PhD's, as well as persons from a pantheon of religions, cultures, races, and ethnic backgrounds. He organized the church; an educated church. An aware church. A church with gifts and skills that were not being used. Same war; different instruments.

Read this carefully: If my students have no interest in what I am teaching, or if your congregation has no interest in what you are preaching, let me assure you it is not because they don't like you nor that they don't love Jesus. Both populations may be rebelling against what we are saying because they are disappointed; they are expecting something different from you, because they are in search of something different from you. Barack Obama discovered just what this generation was seeking and this is it.

- An experience of shared leadership; the notion that one leader and only one is a passing phenomenon. There is a leader in all of us. There is something of value that can be shared by all of us. One "man" can no longer hog the mike!
- All must stand on level ground; there can be no big-shots or little shots, no big I's and little u's.
- Congregations must be invested in coming to terms with social and thorny issues and welcome those who are not like us into the conversation.
- Transparency is the goal. As many as possible must "buy in" to whatever goals and purposes the congregation or community might seek. Diversity is the next-door neighbor to transparency and is there to ensure that all, rich or poor, black or white, Muslim or Christian, Jew or Gentile, have a seat at the welcome table.

Understand that the priorities of this generation and those that are yet to come do not center around place, structures, and buildings. This generation has spawned in their children a disinterest in spending money for grand cathedrals; they prefer to invest their funds in missionary and social programs that will have an immediate impact on those who are the least and the left out among us. So, if your capital campaign fails to produce the funds necessary to build the church of your dreams it was not because you failed to plan but because the plan did not meet the intellectual and spiritual interests of this new generation.

Producing Prophets

If it is true that all the prophets are gone, what is the problem, where did they go? Perhaps, sadly, the problem may be that we have reached the point in our religious history when we are producing preachers but failing to produce prophets; we have preachers a'plenty who speak in terms of personal piety but who fail to be prophets who speak of social responsibility. Some preachers are nothing more than parish priests who tend to the elements at the altar and manage the order of worship and the singing of grand hymns but have abandoned their rightful role as bold spokesmen and women of the living God.

We have preachers, far too many preachers I fear, who are defined and regrettably dismissed as one *"who gives religious advice in a tiresome manner;"* homiletic fluff and theological nonsense. Far too many pulpits are filled with those who specialize in being preachers but who have neither the voice nor the will to be prophets who unashamedly declare God's word with sharpened scalpels of exegetical precision and homiletic care.

There are preachers who will speak with evangelical fervor regarding the great doctrinal watchwords of our faith: sin, judgment, sanctification, justification, atonement and all the rest. But there are not many who search out the oracles of God to declare a word regarding racism, sexism, militarism, peace, justice, and the ethical demands as well as the social imperatives of the Gospel. It may be safe to say, I think, that this generation and those to come are in search of *new watchwords.*

The question persistently dogs us: Where have all the prophets gone?

Is there on the horizon a new Isaiah who, in the face of some earthly Uzziah, will dare to speak of rough places made plain and crooked places made straight?

Is there a Jeremiah, called to his prophetic office while still in his mother's womb, who understands that the authentic prophet is *"set over the nations and over the kingdoms, to root out and to pull down, and to destroy, and to throw down, to build and to plant."?* (1:10)

Is there yet an Ezekiel who understands that a part of his calling is to sit where the refugees sit, to sit among exiles and be astonished by their pain and angered by their suffering, whose prophetic word is so liberating and so resurrecting that dry bones are re-connected and dead men stand on their feet in the cemetery of the slain?

Is there an Habakkuk who in this day will put on the robes of the prophet and declare in the midst of recession, bank bailouts, economic and ecological disasters, political parties and their candidates running amuck who dares to declare: *"Although the fig tree shall not blossom, neither shall fruit be in the vines; the labour of the olive shall fail, and the fields shall yield no meat; the flock shall be cut off from the fold, and there shall be no herd in the stalls, yet I will rejoice in the Lord, I will joy in the God of my salvation! ?" (Habakkuk 3:17-18)*

Are we left to sadly wring our hands in resignation and despair wondering where all the prophets have gone? Or do we dare, like Elisha, call on our seminaries to become rebirthed as a new gathering of the sons and daughters of the Prophets with the bold belief that somehow the mantle of God-kissed speech and anointed proclamation will anoint those who come within theological walls, with a "double portion" of the spirit of God? Could it be that God calls us to give birth to a prophetic culture, a prophetic pedagogy and prophetic mission? But what does that mean?

Prophetic Culture means that our behavior as a community, as the Beloved Community, becomes infectious in terms of what it takes to cultivate a civilization, that is at one with its traditions and values as we stand "sub spacie eternitatus" (Under the gaze of God). even as it gives birth to a wider world of compassion and healing grace. This means that we teach the church and as we disciple the church we will be about the business of demonstrating how the body of Christ infiltrates the culture with prophetic behaviors, deals prophetically with keen insight and collective compassion, and then finds within itself the capacity to be the prophetic church. When one speaks the whole church speaks and all are gifted with an unmistakable fire.

Prophetic Pedagogy means, at the very least, that every seminary take as it purpose for being the development of preachers and prophets who are wedded to the Word. The seminary's purpose for being should be the production of prophets. We cannot hope to produce either preachers or prophets if all that is required is 3 hours for a semester's grade. You can only harvest what you plant. If we are serious and intentional about the formation of prophets, ultimately we shall indeed change the world.

We need look no further than Luke's 4th chapter to see and grasp **Prophetic Mission**; the purpose and charge that is ours.

> *The Spirit of the Lord is upon me*
> *Because He has anointed me*
> *To preach the Gospel to the poor;*
> *He has sent me to heal the brokenhearted,*
> *To proclaim liberty to the captives*
> *And recovery of sight to the blind,*
> *To set at liberty those who are oppressed*
> *To proclaim the acceptable year of the Lord*
> LUKE 4:18FF.

We are in the train of the Prophet Amos. We are not all prophets. Yet we have come to that season where prophets must serve like priests and priests must speak like prophets. We are all not the sons or daughters of prophets. Yet we must come to the place where we view the office of the prophetic not as a noun, the name by which we are called, but as an adjective that describes more fully what we are called to do.

Perhaps we are from the South, some southern city called Tekoa.

Perhaps we are no more than herdsmen of Sycamore trees, gatherers of its fruit.

Perhaps, like Amos, we are living in a nation that is blessed by its prosperity but inwardly idolatrous and morally corrupt.

We shall be prophets not because of our locale nor because of our occupation but because we have received what the late Dr. Peter Marshall called *"a tap on the shoulder,"* a divine summons to speak, an inescapable urge to go, and an inward imperative to give voice to the oracles of the Divine.

The Conclusion of the Whole Matter

The German sociologist, Max Weber, used the terms "priestly and the prophetic" as typologies for ancient Israelite religion and proposed them as concepts which lead to "religious virtuosi," or those who work in the institutions of the Divine. This is useful for us only in our insistence that the priestly and prophetic exercises of ministry are not contradictory. They are, on the contrary, complimentary elements of a synthesis of ministry that must be faithful to the commands of the Eternal.

In similar manner, Dr. Samuel Dewitt Proctor also wrote of this envisioned synthesis when he typified the Black preacher as one who is "Healing priest at one moment and clarion prophet the next."

In these peculiar, stress-filled times, in this mean-spirited culture, we certainly need a priest.

- A priest who will, with dutiful attention, open daily the doors of the temple.
- A priest who will offer at the altar a sacrifice of prayer and praise, a delight for the nostrils of God.
- A priest who will anoint with oil those who are sick and listen with compassion to the confessions of those stained by sin.
- A priest who is the ecclesiastical caretaker who insures that the place of worship is always ready and the order of worship is designed to usher the people of God into the presence of God.

At the same time, we need a prophet. It may well be that the church is in its present state because we have produced far too many preachers but not enough prophets. We need a prophet:

- A prophet who, in the words of Athenagoras in his *Apology* is *"one lifted in ecstasy above the natural operation of their minds by the impulses of the Divine spirit ... inspired to utterance, the Spirit making use of them as a flute-player breathes into his flute."* We need a prophet.
- A prophet who can look backward to see where the footprints of God have been and who is also able to look to see yonder horizon and tell the places where God has promised to show up.

If the church is to be found in an authentically prophetic posture, then there must be a move away from mediocrity in the pulpit. Preaching that would be prophetic must not only include specific expressions of God's will with regard to the church's stance on a particular societal matter, it must also express and proclaim an immanent and immutable God who is always on the side of society's disadvantaged and dispossessed. Prophetic preaching always speaks God's Word and will, concerning the downtrodden and the least among us.

Our challenge, then, is to bring up a generation of priests who preach like prophets and a generation of prophets who serve like priests. "The challenge of the church's intellectuals will be to raise their voice as a trumpet in the cacophony of the public square ... the church must be the voice of conscience that speaks truth to the power of the state, the market, and the body politic, even as it speaks peace to the troubled soul and preaches Good News to the poor."[27]

Finally, this codicil. The Prophet must preach! God requires an authentic prophet. We do not need a "Prof-it" (with an f) to proclaim a gospel of prosperity. We do not need a profit (f) to make of God a "cosmic bellhop who is obliged to give you what you need precisely when you need it."[28]

Those who would preach must never forget that we have only to work with words about the Word. Our words are tied into the concept of what James Earl Massey called "The Preacher's Rhetoric." It was Massey's concern that "preaching demands knowledge of words and how they should be used, how to organize those words under some subject for proper sequence, proportion, unity and clarity.... Rhetoric has to do with intention and design in speaking, a systematic approach by which speaking serves some predeter-

---

27 Callahan, Allen Dwight., "Unpublished Paper on Ordination," Harvard University, July 1997.
28 *Prophetic Business*, Dr. H. Beecher Hicks, Jr., published by Urban Ministries, Inc., 2002.

mined end. Effective preaching has always demanded competence in choosing words and in using them."[29]

The prophet must also understand that rhetoric also requires action; it requires that the prophet or spokesman soil his or her garments with dirt stirred up along the dusty road of life. Your prophetic charge may require a visit to the huts and hovels of Goshen. Your prophetic task may take you on a stroll with Jeremiah through the Potter's House. It may be you'll need to take a detour and sit down on the banks of the Babylon and teach them to sing one of Zion's songs. Your assignment may be to sit with Hosea a spell. He's been having trouble at home, don't you know? My best advice is to know that when the prophetic mantle is upon you, be assured, you're going somewhere.

The prophet must preach and the only thing more tragic than a preacher who *will not* preach is a preacher who *cannot* preach. The preacher who cannot preach is one who has become frightened by the enemy, real or imagined, seen and unseen. This form of preaching is more difficult than you may imagine. God gives God's Word to the prophet and instructs the prophet to share it with those who do not want to see it or hear it. So, if you discover that you are unwilling or unable to perform the function required of you, find another place to be silent. At this juncture of the churches' life,

---

[29] Massey, James Earl, "A Celebration of Ministry: Essays in Honor of Frank Bateman Stanger, The Preacher's Rhetoric," Francis Asbury Publishing Company, Inc., p. 88f.

there is no place for prophets who will not or cannot preach. If yours is not to preach from the pulpit or to prophesy from the public square, then perhaps you will preach from the platform of your secular vocation. God may be calling you to preach as an educator, a designer of digital media, a lawyer, an accountant, a physician; whatever gift God has given you, wherever God has planted you, use that place as a platform on which to preach. Use it to prophesy.

I hear the voice of a young, would-be prophet who has questions to ask, if, as you suggest, there is uncertainty in terms of our calling and if we are beset by the peculiarities of a desacralized culture, what is it that would cause us still to preach?

Since we are called to walk on the pavement of a godless culture and forced to traffic in arenas where we are constantly assaulted by "principalities and powers," by "spiritual wickedness in high places," how shall we dare preach? And just how will we know if we have been called as priests or as prophets?

Prevenient Causality

The answer is to be found in what is called **"prevenient causality."** You will understand what I mean when I point you to Jeremiah's narrative of his own call to ministry. Jeremiah says it happened this way:

> *"Then the Word of the Lord came unto me saying,*
> BEFORE *I formed thee in the belly I knew thee;*
> *And* BEFORE *thou camest forth out of the womb*
> *I sanctified thee,*
> *And I ordained thee a prophet unto the nations."*
> JEREMIAH 1:5

Prevenient causality. The word "prevenient," of course, comes from the Latin *praevenire* which means, quite literally, *that which comes before*. In other words, we preach because of something that comes before. I am aware that western scientific thought would argue that prevenient causality is redundant. That which is the cause of something else must come before it. Yet, it is inescapably true that our God is the cause before the cause. God says: **"BEFORE** I formed thee in the belly...!" "BEFORE you were conceived...!" "BEFORE I took my finger and joined atoms and molecules together to make you, you." God comes BEFORE!

God is still in the prophet-ordaining business. When God decides to make a preacher/prophet it does not occur on the spur of the moment. **Before** the moment of fertilization, **before** the spermatozoon merged with the ovum, God had it all worked out. When prophets are born, it is not the result of some transcendent after-thought.

> God acts before you know God acts.
> God acts before WHEN and prior to WHERE!
>
> God acts beyond the center and the circumference of the orbit of human time.

When someone wants to know when you were called or just when God laid God's hands on you, the answer is "BEFORE!"

> BEFORE the hills in order stood.
> BEFORE the earth received her frame.
> *(from the hymn "O God, Our Help in Ages Past")*
>
> BEFORE the mountains were brought forth.
> *(from Psalm 90:2)*
>
> BEFORE God stretched out the heavens like a curtain above the circle of the earth.
> *(from Isaiah 40:22)*
>
> BEFORE the morning stars sang together or the Sons of God shouted for joy.
> *(from Job 38:7)*

We are where we should be. We shall be what we shall be. Our times are in His hands and at His command. To prophesy or not, it is all in His hands, a process of prevenient causality.

And yet perhaps, like Amos, there can be hope in a herdsman. Perhaps, like Amos, we shall never be professional prophets; but we can know the unmistakable call of God to declare God's unsearchable truth. Perhaps, like Amos, it will be left for us to declare: *"Let justice (judgment) roll down as waters, and righteousness as a mighty stream."* (5:24) God's call is not only for preachers but also for prophets who will speak His word.

> *"Go preach my Gospel," saith the Lord.*
> *"Bid the whole earth my grace receive:"*

He shall be saved that trusts my word,
And he condemned who'll not believe.

"I'll make your great commission known;
and ye shall prove my gospel true
by all the works that I have done,
by all the wonders ye shall do."

"Teach all the nations my commands;
I'm with you till the world shall end;
All power is trusted in my hands: I
can destroy, and I defend." [30]

---

[30] National Baptist Hymn Book, "Go Preach My Gospel (meter hymn)," worded edition, National Baptist Publishing Board, Nashville, TN, 1906, selection 259.

. 4 .

Part II: The Prophetic Pulpit

Proclamation in Perilous Times: The Elijah Paradigm

The great pain of the preaching profession is to find oneself in a weekly search for a sermon. You and I have been there on that strange and peculiar Saturday evening, with no sermon in heart or head, when one waits to hear from heaven or at the very least to hear the flapping of angel's wings in the near distance—preferably with a completed manuscript or an extended outline in their hands. On the other hand, the great joy of the preaching profession is that occasion when, by a gift of extravagant grace, a sermon finds the preacher and the mystical occurs; a Word from high heaven makes its way to low earth through the agency of the human tongue. Unfortunately, that is not always the case.

The greater pain of the preaching profession may be the day one preaches the worst sermon ever to cross the pulpit desk. In truth, most of us who claim to be preachers have known numerous Sundays when our sermonic offerings were feeble at best and, more than likely, an offense to the nostrils of God.

I was licensed to preach on the second Sunday of May, 1961. That was the Sunday I preached my "Initial" or "trial sermon." I did not preach again until the last day of that year when my father, anxious to show off his new preacher, scheduled me to preach the closing sermon of the year—the annual Watch Night Service. After the preaching, on our knees, we prayed the old year out and the new year in. My mother always loved to tell this story of my second sermon—Henry's first (but not last) sermonic disaster.

Everyone in the church building knew that I was headed for disaster with the announcement of my text. It is important to know, however, that I had heard something of the sermon I would preach offered by Dr. Robert Dickerson, Pastor of the St. Paul Church in Pine Bluff, Arkansas. (Beware the temptation to preach another preacher's sermon!) A gifted orator, Dr. Dickerson was able to take difficult texts, wrap them in skilled exegesis as well as living appropriate illustrations, and bring the appreciative congregation regularly to its shouting feet. As I prepared my sermon I heard Dr. Dickerson's words ringing in my head and attempted to commit to memory the salient points of his sermon.

As I stood to preach my misbegotten sermon I guided the congregation to a passage in Psalms that I had never seen before nor have I seen since. Bravely, I announced my sermon topic: MOVING TO THE OUTSKIRTS OF INFINITY! For the next twenty minutes no one knew what in the world I was talking about. I had not figured out what David was talking about; what Robert Dickerson was talking about or what I thought I was talking about. I was forever lost, caught in a time web of the ill prepared and the biblically immature. For the whole time of the sermon a "hush" fell over those crowded pews that by me has been long remembered and never forgotten. Of course, my mother's homiletic evaluation was that I made it to the Outskirts of Infinity and never made it back! It was the one sermon that brought my mother to tears of laughter. Without question, I had preached the worst sermon to ever cross a pulpit desk.

There is a line, a wonderful word of expression that comes out of the crucible of the African American church experience. I remember that every Sunday in the Mount Olivet Church, before the worship would begin, before the worship would begin, the Deacons would always hold "Devotions." We call it "Praise and Worship" now, but where I grew up the Deacons held "Devotions." In the devotional process, somewhere at the end of one of the prayers or at the end of some stirring testimony, (of course, the opening testimony was always something of this variety—someone would begin to sing *"I said I wasn't going to say anything but the Lord has sho' been good to me!"*) Then someone would always add a theological codicil:

> *And for those of you who know*
> *the worth of prayer*
> *- I want you to pray for me -*
> *I want you to pray my strenk (sic) in de Lawd,*
> *An pray that I be the one He be callin' for*
> *In these last and evil days*
> *For these is perlous (sic) times!*

The old folk in Mount Olivet were right; in their time and surely in ours, "these is perlous times." There is a sense of urgency that requires a prophetic pulpit that will not faint nor fear to proclaim the word of God primarily because these is perlous times. These is perilous times, I suspect, because far too often our feeble sermons fail to meet the moment and fail to reflect the mature proclamation our times require. It is to those perilous times that we turn our attention in search of a word of meaning and purpose regarding the prophecy our socio-political disorder demands.

Consider this word taken from the writing of II Kings:

> "And it came to pass, when they were gone over, that Elijah said unto Elisha, ask what I shall do for thee, before I be taken away from thee. And Elisha said, I pray thee, let a double portion of thy spirit be upon me. And he said, thou has asked a hard thing: nevertheless, if thou see me when I am taken from thee, it shall be so unto thee; but if not, it shall not be so. And it came to pass, as they still went

> on, and talked, that behold, there appeared a chariot of fire, and horses of fire, and parted them both asunder; and Elijah went up by a whirlwind into heaven."
> (II KINGS 2:9-11)

This word flows directly from Israel's history, eight centuries before the coming of the Christ. Our attention is secured because of some striking similarities between the time of the text and our own. This is a word that comes from a moment of great peril and transition in the nation's life. Swift were the years of succession that ran between the reign of Ahaziah and the reign of King Jehoram. And through these years the prophet in town was an eccentric prophet, Elijah, the Tishbite.

Immediately, Elijah is described by various biblical exegesis as "the grandest and most romantic character that Israel ever produced." The record of his life confirms that he was the prophet, given to frequent bouts of depression, who declared a three-year drought and while in a dry country found himself fed by ravens day and night somewhere along the banks of the brook Cherith.

They called him names; Ahab especially liked to call him, *"that troubler of Israel."* Elijah was chief antagonist of King Ahab and his Queen, Jezebel. He gained his prophetic reputation that day he conquered and defeated 450 prophets of Baal, while at the same time he was able to call down fire from heaven, a fire hot enough to even make wet wood burn.

You remember him, no doubt because Elijah was the hungry prophet who dined on biscuits and made lunch from a widow woman's languishing oil and disappearing meal in a little out of the way village called Zarephath. In the whole of Israel there had not been a prophet like unto this one called Elijah.

At this point in Israel's history, however, Elijah's days are numbered. God has promised to take Elijah by whirlwind to that land which our foreparents suggest, is a land that is *"fairer than day."* For Elijah there will be no more sudden appearances, no more miracles, and no more tragic conflicts or fiery condemnations. The life of a prophet is about to come to an earthly end.

Before his departure however, Elisha, his constant companion and Prophet-in-Training finds himself in pursuit of his own prophetic credentials. Every time Elijah tries to separate himself from Elisha, Elisha makes it clear that everywhere Elijah is going, he is going. Elijah was an old prophet. Elisha was a would-be, wanna-be prophet. Whether in Bethel where Jacob wrestled with the angel, or in Jericho where at the urging of a unified shout the walls came tumbling down, or down by the River Jordan where Elijah took the mantle of his cloak and divided the waters, there to walk across on dry ground—wherever Elijah went Elisha was sure to follow.

This is, first of all, a word to "old prophets." Let me remind you that if you are an Elijah, if you are the prophet of God you claim to be, be careful where you go, be careful of the soil on which you place your sandals because somewhere there is a young preacher, an Elisha who is following you. Be clear: someone is following you who will imitate you, speak as you speak and live as you live. They will follow your model, your example and may indeed become the preacher/prophet you wanted to be, but never were.

This is, second of all, a word to those young, would-be prophets. Let me remind you that if you seek to have a ministry of substance and significance there is someone in front of you who has already been where you are trying to go. My suggestion is, no matter how smart and gifted you are, if you want the spirit of God in your ministry, you need to find some Elijah, some bearded and bespectacled preacher/prophet who knows the way, and then become aligned and in-line, and follow the prophet God has so clearly placed in your life.

Now comes the moment. After all of his experiences with Elijah, after all of the days in which he has served at Elijah's beck and call, Elijah raises the question: Elisha what do you want? Elisha I can't turn without stumbling all over you. Elisha whatever it is that you want, just ask for it.

> *"Ask what I shall do for thee,*
> *before I be taken away from thee."*

That was the question Elisha had been waiting for. Elisha had been hanging around for a long time just waiting on that question. And you remember what Elisha said—

"Let a double portion of thy spirit be upon me."

I believe that Elisha was on to something. His question was neither ill-timed nor ill-conceived. His request for a "double portion" was not as it may upon first glance appear, a selfish or self serving request. Elisha was not asking for twice as much of Elijah's prophetic gift. Elisha was not asking for more power than was resident in Elijah's ministry. What he was really asking for was the inheritance of the eldest son.

Follow the logic of the story. As I understand it, the eldest son stands in relationship to the father and, therefore, receives an inheritance that might not otherwise fall to his lot.

This is the way it works: I am my father's child! I have what I have not because I deserve it but because I am the son of my father. I am who I am not because I accidentally showed up or because I have "skills." I am who I am because of a God-ordained, genetic DNA process that has ordained that what was in my father is now in me. What my father owned I now own. It is my inheritance, my birthright, the gift of my father's blood, handed down generations to generations that cannot by human hands be taken away.

I will become what I will become not simply because of my own effort and ingenuity but because my father has made preparation for me and has something stored up for me which I cannot secure for myself.

The influence that Elisha would have among other prophets would not come because of his own prophetic prowess, as with Elijah but because somebody could see in him the overflow of prophetic power that came because of his bio-spiritual relationship with Elijah. My blessings come not because of me, but in spite of me. What I have now, however, is not enough. And that is why what I need is a "double portion."

It is critical that preachers learn the deeper meaning of the Elijah-Elisha paradigm. Elisha's request was for more than a double portion of his inheritance. What he asked for was a kind of second anointing, double portion of Elijah's "spirit."

Spirit. The notion of the Spirit is part of the indefinable and the intangible. Spirit. It looks like the prophetic is undergirded by this mystifying thing called "Spirit." I cannot touch it but I can feel it. If you do not understand it, do not despair. That is why the Apostle Paul said that there are some who are set apart to be "stewards of the mysteries of God." Somehow, Elisha knew that something was missing in his life spiritually. Says Elisha, what I really need is something you have. I need more of it than you can imagine. I don't know what you call it—you can call it charisma, you can call it prophetic appeal, your divine endowment or you can call it your anointing. But by whatever name it is known, I need a double portion of your spirit.

Here is the reason I need a double portion. I need it. And if you hope to be pastor, priest, preacher or prophet you will need it as well. When I think of what will be required for ministry in this generation, **I am convinced that we are going to need something extra.** What pastoral ministry, indeed what the prophetic ministry requires today is quite different from what that ministry required a generation ago.

The phenomena I see in the pews on Sunday morning is quite different from what I saw twenty-five years, twenty, even ten years ago. Pews may be filled but those who fill them appear to have no power. Not in every church but in too many churches I see the disinterested, indifferent, unexcited, and bored to death.

Those who come to church may have Bibles in their hands but ours is an age where the level of biblical illiteracy is nothing short of astounding.

Those who come to church are *"in the house"* but the church has become nothing more than spiritualized entertainment; a place to get your shout on but there is nothing left to live on when they get home.

So what we have now is a generation of folk who will do anything and everything in the House of God.

There are those who shop around for the church of their choice or flip channels, or scout out social media or Sunday morning live-streaming until they find something that suits their need for a minute.

It is important to know your audience; that is, to know the character of those to whom you speak. Across the years of this ministry, I know I have preached to those who have multiplied their possessions but reduced their values. Prophet or not, we preach to big men with small characters, to those who earn steep profits but who maintain shallow relationships.

You will preach to a generation of *"church attenders"* who cannot sing the hymns of our faith because they have thrown the hymnbook in the trash bin of liturgical irrelevance, preferring a kind of "Hip-Hop Gospel" that very often has no basis in sound doctrine. Instead of singing hymns we are left to sing 7/11 songs—we sing seven words and then repeat the refrain seven times.

You will preach to a generation of "church members" who will attract politicians to their pulpits but the politicians very often are visitors who are lost once inside and who, when in the course of their discourse, direct worshippers to ***"Two Corinthians."***

Every preacher-prophet among us will preach to congregations who want "pretty preachers" who preach "feel good" sermons that have nothing whatsoever to do with the *"faith once delivered to the saints."* You will preach to those who come to church for the singing but who never managed to get saved.

That is why what I used to do will not work. Yesterday's methodology for ministry is insufficient. The power of the prophetic is endangered and what I used to have in order to justify my prophetic claims is not enough. What used to be enough to get by yesterday will be found insufficient for those of this generation who would redefine the church, forget the commandments, blow off the Beatitudes and dismiss the name of Jesus and His Cross from the marquee of the building. Our survival is at stake. What we will need is a double portion!

This is the implication of what I have been writing. **Not only does this generation require more of those who are engaged in ministry, but what is required is a ministry that is qualitatively and substantively different.**

This is my argument: if the modern pastorate is to be liberated in any sense, if those who claim the mantle of ministry are in any measure to be found prophetic, then it must be liberated from the curse of mediocrity. If the modern pastorate is to be liberated, it must be liberated from the stigma of the shallow and the pursuit of the unimportant.

The great scourge of the church is that far too much of what we call ministry is mired in tradition, in the ordinary and the common place. We do what we do this year because that's the way we did it last year. Look at our churches. By and large, there is nothing new. No new outlooks. No new perspectives. Just the "same old, same old." On any given Sunday nothing new is done and no new word is proclaimed. To see what occurs in most of our churches in the name of preaching would lead us to believe that God has abandoned the prophetic process and is off looking for someone else God can call to preach. And then we wonder why nobody stays with the church.

If the church is to be found in an authentically prophetic posture then there must be a move away from mediocrity in the pulpit. It bears repeating: Preaching that would be prophetic must not only include specific expressions of God's will with regard to the church's stance on a particular societal matter; it must also express and proclaim an immanent and immutable God who is involved on the side of society's disadvantaged and dispossessed. Prophetic preaching always speaks God's word and will on behalf of the downtrodden. That is why the words of Dr. Gardner Taylor are so critically important:

> "The preaching that gets closest to the throbbing heart
> of God is preaching that rises out of circumstances
> touched and tinged with heartbreak, heartbreak that
> sees and senses and says something
> of the heartbreak of God, which is undaunted
> by resistance and opposition, and which marches
> resolutely by way of a cross on a hill to shout
> in a cemetery." [31]

---

31 Martha Simmons and Frank A. Thomas, "Preaching with Sacred Fire: An Anthology," W. W. Norton and Co., New York, NY, p. 21, The Foreword by Gardner Taylor

Women In Ministry

Yet another dimension with respect to Black preaching draws our attention. Just what is the role of women in the African American pulpit? I have devoted a significant portion of my ministry to the liberation of Black women into the ordained ministry. Regrettably, far too many women are yet excluded from positions of pastoral leadership. Bishop Leontine T. C. Kelly in her essay on *The Woman as Preacher*, speaks to this issue thoughtfully and thoroughly:

> "The Black woman preacher ... battles sexism, but she draws upon the spiritual confidence traditionally in her culture. She is theologically and experientially grounded in a God who is Creator and Sustainer of the universe, actively holding the "whole world in her hands." She draws her understanding of a father/mother God from the traditional expression of the spiritual of her people, "He's my father, He's my mother, my sister and my brother, he's everything to me. The good news of the gospel of Jesus Christ is liberating from every societal binding. There is no way for a Black woman to have understood the Christian witness of her people, who received the message of salvation from the very persons who enslaved them, without affirming her personhood sexually as well as racially." [32]

---

[32] Kelly, Leontine T. C., "The Woman as Preacher in Women Ministers," Judith L. Weidman, Harper and Row, San Francisco, 1971, p. 72.

In like manner, Dr. Cheryl Sanders speaks of the similarities and differences in the preaching of men and women. She concludes that "women and men preach the same types of sermons, from the biblical texts, but differ slightly in their choices of themes and tasks, and differ greatly in their talk about God and persons in inclusive terms. Perhaps we can say that women and men preach the same Word but with distinctive accents—women tend to emphasize the personal, and men the prophetic ... Yet it may be that this small discrepancy between women's and men's preaching holds the key to a possible resolution of this dichotomy in our own age of rapid social and cultural change." Sanders goes on to say that "women's sermons can teach men to temper social criticism with compassion. At the same time women can learn from men how to sharpen their own testimonies and calls for Christian commitment with the cutting edge of prophetic indignation."[33]

> *A Story Worth Reading!*
> *(The names have been changed to protect the innocent.)*
>
> *Whether this story is fact or fable, truth or fiction, I shall never tell. The lessons taught, however, are real. In the summer of 1977 a preacher came to town. Eyes wide with anticipation for the ministry journey that lay before him, the young preacher could taste the growth the church was destined to know.*

---

33 Sanders, Cheryl J., "African American Religious Studies: An Interdisciplinary Anthology, The Woman as Preacher," Gayraud, Wilmore (ed.), Duke University Press, Durham and London, 1989 , p. 373ff.

All went well for the first few years until that day she knocked at his office door. Bright eyed, she was only a whisper of a young woman but she had a burden and shared it with her pastor. It was not long before she was permitted to "confess" her call and to preach her "trial" sermon. Several years later she was ordained to the gospel ministry. With appropriate ceremony, hands were laid on her and she was given both hymnal and Bible as the sword and shield she would need for ministry in days to come.

Then the letter came ... from a gathering of pastors and preachers across town, a meeting of ministers ... The room was small but packed; more preachers than seats.

"Sir: Please present yourself at meeting time and place to show good cause why you should not be expelled from your membership of the gathering of Pastors. By now you should know we do not permit women to preach in our churches."

To which came the reply: Sirs, "if you will show me in this Bible where I have erred I shall make a public apology but I cannot permit tradition and sexism to prevent women from fulfilling the requirements of their God given call."

The response: "We're not talking about the Bible." And in reply, "Sirs, if we are not talking about the Bible we have no basis for discussion!"

Consequentially, the young preacher was put out, expelled, summarily dismissed, cut off from the "fellowship" of the brethren. All because she was a woman!

> *Since that day over 200 persons have been licensed, ordained and/or installed into the Gospel ministry by that church, the majority of which are women while most have completed their theological training.*
> **Ain't God a wonder! ? Ain't God a Woman? Ain't that good news! ?**

We are caught, then, in the strangling webs of our own traditions, failing to see that those very traditions, including discrimination against women have turned off a generation; consequently, the folk we used to preach to are not there anymore. The church, black and white, appears to have been marginalized into irrelevance. The church appears to have lost its power to transform the culture. The church watched in horror and disbelief while the campaign for the nation's highest office unleashed a racist, sexist, xenophobic, misogynistic sub-culture that political parties cannot contain and to which the Church of Jesus Christ has failed to speak. Even the African American Church appears to have lost its moral high ground and is no longer the redemptive and socially salvific force it had once become.

And so, Prophet of God, here we are—trapped by mediocre thinking, mediocre planning, untenable biases, and mediocre strategies stirred in a dangerously polluted and poisonous pot, spoiled by feckless preaching that is absent any semblance of the appearance of the Holy Spirit. We're in trouble and don't even know it.

We claim we have a Great Commission to evangelize the world and yet we lack the strength to evangelize the neighborhood. Gentrification has done great harm, particularly to inner city churches with a lack of off-street parking making the church increasingly vulnerable to new neighbors who have no need for churches in their neighborhood. The neighbors then quickly mobilize their complaint to City Hall to impose severe and restrictive parking regulations, thus impacting the revenue needed to sustain ministries that have provided a multitude of services, some for over 100 years. We claim we are Chosen Disciples tasked to do business in great waters when, in fact, we are sinking in shallow waters while we merrily float our sailboats in ecclesiastical bathtubs.

Still there is yet another reason why Elisha required a double portion. I suspect that Elisha was on to something and that he was really seeking to insure his own prophetic authenticity. In his pursuit of the prophetic mantle of Elijah, he may have suspected that the day would dawn when there would be a shortage of authentic prophets.

Young preacher, you must pay attention. I did not say that the day would dawn when there would be a shortage of preachers; what I said was that the day would dawn when there would be a shortage of prophets. Preachers are a dime a dozen but where are the prophets?

- Where are the prophets who counsel kings at the peril of their own safety?

- Where are the prophets who "cry loud and spare not"?
- Where are the prophets who, like Ezekiel, stand in the gap; who speak and dead men live?
- Where are the prophets who dare shake their fists at Congress and dare point a prophetic finger toward Pennsylvania Avenue?

The Authentic Prophet

God requires an authentic prophet and that is why Elisha understood that in order to insure his own authenticity, in order to insure his relevance and his viability, he did not need something superficial, he did not need something on the surface; what he required was a double portion!

The writing must not stop here. I suspect danger in this Elijah-Elisha paradigm. Be careful when you ask for a double portion. When you ask for a double portion you could be headed for double trouble.

Do not think that this prophetic profession is an easy one. Do not be too swift to judge or seek to wear another's pulpit gown.

Do not be misled by the glamour and the glitz of what you see some other Elijah do and come to think that you have a right to be there, with no sweat of effort on your brow, to claim their prize.

No doubt Elisha had seen Elijah stop up the heavens and prevent rain, call down fire from heaven, and pray until a dead boy got back on his feet. Ah, but that's what you saw on the outside.

You must never forget that Elijah had to spend some time under a juniper tree, or that he had to spend some down time dealing with his own demons of personal doubt and depression. Never forget that Elijah had to spend time with his own sense of aloneness and frustration and personal, psychological pain, his own brand of *PPTSD (Post Pastoral Traumatic Syndrome Disease)*. That fight Elijah had with Ahab and his wife Jezebel was more than a school yard skirmish.

I don't mean to burst your bubble but in this thing called pastoral ministry there is some pain. There's some heartbreak here. There's some sadness here. *"Preaching Through a Storm"* is not merely a metaphor. Storms do rage. Winds do blow. The forces of nature will beat against your face. The very agents of Satan and agents of Hell itself, and evil, unclean spirits are in some of these churches today. So, before you decide you want to be a prophet, before you decide you want a "double portion" of something your Elijah has, please understand that it is possible that you will get what you ask for, but you will also get double for your trouble.

In pursuit of the prophetic, Elisha asked Elijah for a double portion. But there's trouble ahead. This is the trouble. Every Elisha that follows an Elijah ought beware the temptation of ministry with another prophet's anointment. There is nothing inherently wrong with seeing an Elijah in your life who becomes a role model for your ministry. We learn by doing as others have done and profit greatly by the example of those who have gone before us. Nevertheless, the authentic prophet validates that authenticity only to the extent that he or she operates out of an anointment that is his or hers alone. You must be careful with someone else's anointment.

Let me see if I can make this plain. This will make you laugh. One of the gifts of the African American preaching tradition is something called the "whoop." Now, let me tell you! **I do not understand the prejudicial unfairness of God in that some have been given this gift while others of us have not.** And while I have been preaching this gospel for more than fifty years, for all of those years I have been in search of a whoop. I want to be able to get that sweetness in my throat, that special timbre of voice that makes the sermon lyrical and hauntingly sweet. But I don't have it. I want to be able to lay my head back and let all the tonal qualities of my vocal chords blend into a melodic climax for my sermon. But, sad to say, I don't have it.

In her writing on WHOOPING: THE MUSICALITY OF AFRICAN AMERICAN PREACHING PAST AND PRESENT, Martha Simmons helps us clarify the meaning and nature of the art. Says Simmons:

> "Whooping can be thought of as parallel to great opera. The tonality enhances the beauty as well as

> *the depth of impact. The hearer is caught up in the sermon, as one may be caught up in the dramatic power of an opera, because of the combined impact of tone and word...Whooping is first melody, that can be identified by the fact that its pitches are logically connected and have prescribed, punctuated rhythms that require certain modulations of voice, and is often delineated by quasi-metrical phrasings.*
>
> SIMMONS, SACRED FIRE, P. 865

More to the point, both the "tune" and the "whoop," when entered into the sermon with integrity and without the purpose of showing off or show-boating, can be a significant addition to the sermon and its acceptance by the waiting congregation. The whoop adds spacing, timing, syncopation, beat, melody, and drama to the sermon. When first heard, the whoop will be hard to understand and accept. Over-time it will be appreciated for the gift it truly is.

And the one thing I have discovered is that the worst thing you can ever do is try to whoop when you don't have a whoop. That which was intended as a serious spiritual gift can quickly erode and the preacher becomes the target of ridicule and scorn.

Do not misunderstand me, I can whoop. In the shower, I have an awesome whoop. In my car, by myself, I can whoop until the dashboard shouts. But on Sunday morning, when it counts, my whoop deserts me and *"I am of all men most miserable."*

And every once in a while a preacher would come by Metropolitan with a certified whoop and I would take him in the confidence of my inner chamber and tell him that I would make a significant contribution to his personal wealth that day if he would just teach me how to whoop. But I'm here years later to tell you I still can't whoop. I have discovered that even if I try to whoop like someone else whoops, it's just not my whoop. Heed this warning; if you don't have it, don't try it!

And that's the way it is with an anointing. What I am in search of is not an anointment that is *on* me; I am in search of an anointment that is *in* me. I am in search of an anointment that empowers me to seek and to accomplish that which is in me, that which is authentic and real.

Here's the problem. When I take on someone else's anointment, when I exercise a gift that is not uniquely and singularly my own, I am merely engaged in an "event." An event is something that occurs once and is over. An event is entertainment. An authentic prophetic anointment is something that occurs even when you don't know it is occurring. I can hear William Jones, (known by his own admission to practice his preaching and his whoop while tending the cars in the motor pool while serving his stint in the Army) now bellowing in Bethany, "What I've got wasn't handed down; I didn't take preaching up, it took me up. I was God called. I am God sent. I'm not here by personal prerogative. I'm here by divine determination." I said, 'I don't want something *on* me; I want something *in* me."

So, then, if you are in pursuit of the prophetic, there are things you need to understand about this prophetic anointment. Look at the text again:

> *"And Elisha said, I pray thee, let a double portion of thy spirit be upon me. And he said, thou hast asked a hard thing: nevertheless, if thou see me when I am taken from thee, it shall be unto thee; but if not, it shall not be so."*
> II KINGS 2:9FF.

First of all, a prophetic anointment cannot be given to you. Elijah could not give what he had to Elisha. That's why Elijah responded to Elisha, what you have asked is *"a hard thing."* I cannot give to you what first had to be given to me. I cannot give you what I did not possess in the first place. Nobody but God can give you what you need and what God wants you to have. He who calls you will also equip you.

Nobody but God can set your preaching tongue on fire. Nobody but God can take the coals from Isaiah's altar and place them on your lips. Nobody but God can give you Jeremiah's fire and then shut it up in your bones. Nobody but God, in the words of James Weldon Johnson, can *"Put (your) eye to the telescope of eternity, and let (you) look upon the paper walls of time." Nobody but God can "turpentine your imagination and put perpetual motion in your arms and then set your arms on the pinwheels of eternity."*[34] Nobody but God can anoint your head with oil and then arrange for your cup and your saucer to run over as well.

Second of all, the thing you need to understand is that in pursuit of the prophetic, **whatever your anointment is, it is always in connection with an assignment.** Your car needs oil not because you like Exxon or because you have a business deal with the oil barons of Saudi Arabia, but because you are going somewhere! Elisha would be anointed because he had a job to do; he was going somewhere.

Elisha's assignment was to follow Elijah. Not only that, Elisha's assignment was to pour water on Elijah's hands (2 Kings 3:11). What it means is that every time Elijah went to the bathroom Elisha was there to help him wash his hands. I'm talking about being a servant. Elisha's assignment would require him to be involved in the nastiness, the grit and grime of ministry.

Elisha's assignment was to be a servant.

There is no prophetic anointment apart from service. Your anointment is an invitation to serve before you lead. Your anointment is certification that you have been through the trenches and the trials, enough wind and rain, that God says you are authorized as God's Ambassador. I say again that the path to power leads through the latrine; the path to power leads

---

34 Johnson, James Weldon, "God's Trombones: Seven Negro Sermons in Verse," Viking Press, NY, p. 14., 1927

through the servant's quarters! If you want an anointing, help somebody.

Your anointing, your power, your gift is always in direct proportion to your willingness to serve.

Listen to Elisha's words:

> "And Elisha said, I pray thee, let a double portion of thy spirit be upon me. And he said, Thou has asked a hard thing: nevertheless, if thou see me when I am taken from thee, it shall be unto thee; but if not, it shall not be so."

Do not forget that Elijah could not give Elisha his spirit or his anointing. To do so, says Elijah, would be "a hard thing." What he said to him was that he needed to stay with him in order that he could see him taken away and then his request would be granted. In other words, I can't give it to you but if you put yourself in the right place, you'll get what you're looking for.

In this ministry business, all God wants is to get you in the right place so that you can be used in the way that He wants to use you. You don't understand why God keeps on moving you from place to place, from church to church, always living in tents, always on the move, never in a permanent location; but all God wants to do is to get you in the right spot. God wants to get you in the right position because there's a lesson God needs to teach; there's some instruction God wants to give. There's a blessing waiting for you but God's got to get you positioned under an open window so you can receive it. God wants to get you in the place that is designed not for you, nor by you, but for God to gain the glory.

I have decided wherever God wants me, I'll go. Is that your decision? Wherever He can use me, wherever God leads me, it will be all right. As long as God gets the glory... as long as God gets the praise... as long as God gets the honor, wherever God wants me, wherever God leads me, I'll go.

Do not forget that when Elisha asked of Elijah a "double portion" he was asking that something would be transmitted from one generation to the next. It looked like—it only looked like—Elisha was asking for something selfish or for something he should not have requested but I believe Elisha was right. There are some things that need to be transferred from generation to generation. There are some values that my ancestors had that my children would do well to have as their own. There are some behaviors that yesterday's generation had that this generation would do well to imitate. There are some methods that my father had that I need to employ right now. Some things need to be transferred from generation to generation.

The reason things need to be transferred from generation to generation is because some things never change. I don't care how young you are one day you're going to need some old things. I don't care how attracted you are to the things that are new; one day you will realize that the things that will hold you are the things that are old.

Some things never change. The Word of God never changes. *"The grass withers, the flower fades but the Word of our God shall stand forever."*

Some things never change. The Bible never changes. I don't know about you but I'm still preaching the Bible. I'm not preaching out of the text book, I'm not preaching out of the newspaper. I am not preaching out of theological journals. I am, however, preaching from the entrails of a human heart that knows what it is to hurt and to bleed, a human heart besieged and beset by the trials and struggles of my anxious faith. Sometime up, sometime down but I'm still preaching the Bible. I still believe *"the Holy Bible was written by men divinely inspired and is a perfect treasure of heavenly instruction; that it has God for its author, salvation for its end, and truth without any mixture of error for its matter..."*[35]

Some things never change. God never changes. My Bible tells me He changes not. God is unalterable because He is from Everlasting to Everlasting. *"There is one and only one living and true God; an infinite intelligent spirit whose name is Jehovah, the maker and supreme ruler of heaven and earth, inexpressibly glorious in holiness and worthy of all possible honor, confidence and love."*[36]

Let me remind you that the prophet is first and foremost a preacher. Did I tell you that these is (sic)

---

[35] National Baptist Convention, Statement on Religious Freedom, Julius R. Scruggs, President, June 21, 2012.
[36] The New National Baptist Hymnal, National Baptist Publishing Board, Nashville, TN, 1977, pgs 606-609.

"perlous" times? In these "perlous" times it is required that the prophet preach. Far too many of us, however, have been infected with what I call "Prophetic laryngitis." The hungry and homeless are dying on street corners. Preach, prophet.

The blood of our children is running in the sewers and the streets. Preach, prophet. You will never be popular but you will also never escape from the imperative to preach. Preach, prophet! Preach.

Whatever you have—pass it on. Whatever God has put in you, share it with someone else—pass it on. Whatever blessing God has given you—pass it on. Whatever Spirit God has invested in you—pass it on. Whatever hope is in you—pay it forward, pass it on. It's not yours anyhow so, pass it on!

Let me pass something on to you. Let me take a personal moment. I want to help you understand that the path of the prophetic is never easy and your way will never be plain. In 1961 I was a freshman student at Wittenberg University in Springfield, Ohio. It was in the spring of the year, when a sense of the "urgency of God" came into my life and I was convinced that I was called to preach. Not knowing where to go or to whom I could turn for immediate clarification regarding what I was sensing, I turned to the Dean of the Hamma Divinity School.*

I shall never forget that bright spring morning as I entered into his office nurturing the twin emotions of excitement and fear. And after I told the Dean my story he suggested that my feelings were not necessarily related to a "call" and perhaps I needed to rethink the matter. No word of encouragement. No word of direction. No word of support or inspiration. I was, as Paul put it, "cast down but not destroyed!" It was clear to me as I stood in the Dean's office that no mantle, no portion, certainly no double portion would ever fall on my shoulders.

But now, more than *fifty-five years later*, I have the grace to thank the Dean. I want to thank the Dean because he let me know I would not make it on an easy road.

I want to thank him because he let me know I would not make it without opposition.

I want to thank the Dean because he let me know that I would not make it because of my name or because of the genes from which I had come.

I want to thank the Dean because I now know what obviously the Dean did not know: **"God can raise up a nobody from nowhere and put the truth in his heart and words on his lips."** I want to thank the Dean because when he thought I was nobody that's when God decided to make me somebody! And there's nothing the Dean can do about it.

And that's why I can write these words to you now to keep on preaching. When the world says, "sit down!" keep on preaching. When the world says, "shut up!" keep on preaching. Preach the whole counsel of God. Preach the Word. When men turn you away and slam the door in your face, preach the Word. "In season and out," preach the Word!

Do not forget that when Elisha, standing on Jordan's banks, saw the very presence of God, the scripture says that Elijah was taken "up by a whirlwind into heaven." He or she who lives in pursuit of the prophetic, he or she who lives in the full flow of the prophetic tradition, will one day stand in the whirlwind of God and feel for yourself the spray of the morning mists upon your face.

That God-kissed whirlwind that says things are about to change.

That God-ordained whirlwind that says that Kronos will be caught up into Kairos.

That God-directed whirlwind that dictates the terms and time of my departure.

I do not know when.

But one day I shall stand in the very winds of God.

One day I shall stand in some gentle zephyr there to be transported to the throne room of God there to hear my Savior's voice. Winds.

- Winds shall carry me yonder...
- Winds shall take me from the shores of time to the shores of eternity...
- Winds that shall carry me to the Eternal's throne in that city that lies four square.
- I do not know when but I know my wind is coming!

- I shall not die. My wind is coming.
- I shall be changed. My wind is coming.
- I shall be translated. My wind is coming.
- In a moment, in the twinkling of an eye, my wind is coming.
- I shall be liberated. My wind is coming.

Swing down, chariot,
Stop and let me ride!
Swing low, sweet chariot,
Coming for to carry me home.
I looked over Jordan and what did I see?
A band of angels coming after me.
Coming for to carry me home!

Author to Reader:

Throughout the lifting of the ideas regarding the Prophetic Pulpit it seems reasonable to ask what Prophetic Preaching looks like, feels like. What kind of parameters contain this form of preaching? How is it done? Is there a setting in which it is appropriate and another when it is not? In July of 2016, at the meeting of the Democratic National Convention, Rev. Dr. William Barber came to the stage with words that fairly teemed with the prophetic. ADDENDUM 1 is the written manuscript of his sermon. In a word, this is what prophetic preaching is all about!

. 5 .

Part III: The Prophetic Pulpit

Preaching While Bleeding

> "And lest I should be exalted above measure through the abundance
>
> Of the revelations, there was given to me A thorn in the flesh..."
>
> (II COR. 12: 7-8)

There is a legend about a Thorn Bird that sings just once in its life, more sweetly than any other creature on the face of the earth. From the moment it leaves the nest it searches for a Thorn Tree and does not rest until it has found one. Then, singing among the savage branches, it impales itself upon the longest, sharpest spine. And, dying, it rises above its own agony to out-carol the Lark and the Nightingale. The whole world stills to listen and God in His heaven smiles. For the best is only bought at the price of great pain!

— COLLEEN MCCULLOUGH, *The Thorn Birds*

A Word of Clarification:
Is there a Prophet in the house?

While the subject of this writing may be shocking if not off-putting for some, the reality is that the preacher/prophet and the church must have the necessary resources to restore the ethical values, principled ideals, and spiritual principles which have been the foundation upon which this nation and our lives have been based and blessed. Additionally, the poetic recital regarding the "Thorn Bird" admittedly is based on legend; of course there is always some question about the truth of such legends. Nevertheless, I invite you to be open to the metaphor and to the lessons the "Thorn Bird" imparts.

The question we must face at the outset has to do with the source of the bleeding and the impact such bleeding has upon our lives. Truth be told there are inescapable forces and sources that have changed our communities, changed the political landscape, and changed the willingness at least to preach if not to be prophetic within it. That is why these random writings of mine may be important for those who are called to ministry as well as to those who are not. What are those forces and sources? There are several:

First, the cataclysmic changes in the political landscape. Traditional and conventional political leadership has been thoroughly abandoned. With the landslide election of Donald Trump as President of the

United States, heads are turning if not spinning wondering just what the end will be. It is clear that our worlds have been turned upside down and the path forward is anything but clear. Is there a prophet in the house?

Second, the rise of unremitting and undeniable racism. Many thought that with the election of Barack Obama to the Presidency, racism as we had known it would no longer be the thorny problem that it had been for generations. Unfortunately, not so. The problem continues. Gentrification, gerrymandering, and redlining continue. The assault on voting rights continues and with the confirmation of Senator Jeff Sessions to be Attorney General of the United States, prospects of the government as protector of the rights of all has become, at the least, questionable. Hate crimes and countless experiences of personal acts of violence are widespread. Not to mention the unashamed public appearance of racist groups such as the KKK in the public square portend an unhealthy and dark future for a nation espousing "freedom and justice for all."

STOP THE PRESSES

I am glued to my television screen. I cannot believe what I am seeing, but I cannot deny the truth which the nation can no longer deny. There is blood in the streets of Charlottesville, Virginia. Nearby the campus of the University of Virginia, an armed rebellion has a nation horrified by what it sees. A rally was arranged by *Alt-Right* headed by Jason Kessler and white nationalists, ostensibly for the purpose of reclaiming America. They were all there—neo-Nazis, white supremacists, fascists, and of course, the Ku Klux Klan, all the while displaying hand-made signs of hate and waving Confederate flags. The supremacists called their rally, "*Unite the Right.*"

On the other side were the anti-supremacists, *Black Lives Matter*, and a hand-full of clergy whose intent was to register simply by their presence and their voice, opposition to the ill-begotten and public demonstration of bigotry and racial hatred. The whole matter rested on the thin purpose of objection to the removal of a statue of Robert E. Lee from Emancipation Park.

The result was disastrous. What the gathering achieved was to instill fear and distrust in the nation. Such fear was well founded as the number of persons injured began to climb. On the night before, these nationalists, the Klan who marched unashamedly without hoods or masks, paraded in the streets with Tiki Torches—a throwback to the days of slavery and beyond when Blacks were intimidated by the burning of crosses. What they hoped to achieve was the intimidation of black and white clergy and Jewish Rabbi who, despite the despicable methods of the Klan, et al., showed up for the rally anyhow. In truth, it all amounted to a painful display of rage, hate, and death.

Is it any wonder then that our times demand a prophet? We are disappointed (but not surprised) that the voice of moral leadership was not heard from the microphones of the White House. Our *Tweeter-in-Chief* had absolutely nothing to repudiate the actions of these organized racists. His silence is despicable and sends a clear signal to the citizens of the United States and to the world that under "Trumpian" leadership supremacists will have carte blanche within these shores and armed rebellion will be an inescapable reality. I suppose that is why David Duke thought it important to remind Mr. Trump who voted him into office and who did not.

We must cry out again that the principles upon which this nation was founded—that all men are created equal—must be protected by every ounce of our collective strength. Ours must be the voice of dissent that insists on change, and renewal based on love. Our first call must be a

Call to Prayer in the spirit of II Chronicles 7:14. Chronicles assures us that if we pray God's eyes will be open; God's ears will be attentive. Our second call may well be "A call to arms" We must be, in the words of the Prophet Isaiah, "Repairers of the breach" before the walls come tumbling down around us! And if we don't act, we might well be witnessing the death of democracy.

Men and women of goodwill are now summoned to the fore of leadership, charged with the responsibility of speaking to these times and to persons empowered to speak, with lucidity and moral clarity.

So, then, let me speak. How long can we last with leadership that stretches from the ignorant to the insane? How long can we endure the antics of a man who says he wants to make America great but he does so with methods that are offensive to the ear and damaging to the nation. This president takes two days to call evil by its name in Charleston. How long can our nation survive with leadership in the White House who threatens nuclear war abroad but says nothing and does nothing at all about domestic terrorism at home? That's insane.

We must not suffer fools. The die is cast. The future of our nation and our world is clearly at hand. Unless a Prophet comes—and soon—we all shall bleed, a bleeding unto death. Martin Luther King, Jr. was right: "We must learn to live together as brothers or we shall perish together as fools."

Third, the problem of economic disparity. Unfortunately, the economic future continues to be grim as "the past has become prologue"—the rich will continue to be rich and the poor will continue to be poor. The poor will continue to beg bread while the rich will enjoy tax breaks. One tenth of the population controls 90% of the nation's wealth—we think. Healthcare is about to be ripped from under the sick and 20 million people will have "no man" to lift them out of their Bethesda Pool of despair. And they tell me all this is necessary to make America great again. Really? Is there a prophet in the house?

These are but a few of the factors that have had and will continue to have impact on those who would address, change, or even prophesy in the first quarter of the twenty-first century. These choices and resources, in relation to preachers and prophets, are at best external forces that can have major impact on the nature of the programmatic response ministries must make if they are to remain relevant and viable as we seek the way forward. These are the factors that make us bleed collectively; in a sense we all remain victims of the carnage to come. Is there a prophet in the house?

To be fair in this analysis, the forces and sources that impact the culture externally find their way to have impact on the preacher/prophet within the community internally. In this respect, the old adage remains true: "the chickens will come home to roost!" So with what are we faced? What's on the Pastor's plate?

What's happening in the world that soils the prophet's garments? Just what are the things, specifically, that make the preacher bleed while preaching? There are several:

What Makes Us Bleed

First, the instability of the church. I tread on treacherous terrain here but I think it is clear that there is undeniable instability within the Lord's Church. Instability such that we have not yet come to agreement on what the church is or to a clear definition of its meaning and purpose. How many versions and translations of scripture must we have before we can agree on the nature of sin and salvation, righteousness and deliverance, life and death?

How long must we struggle before we reach consensus on who and how one gives leadership to the church? Why is it we are still caught up in doctrinal disputes, unable to agree on the most fundamental principal: "A new commandment I give unto you, that you love one another even as I have loved you"? (John 13:34) How long will our churches remain so insular and self-serving that they would dare declare who can and who cannot become "Disciples of the Way"?

Second, a fundamental distrust of church leadership. As we shall see later, the disappearance of persons in ordained leadership positions is epidemic. This is an intrinsically personal matter, but those who are sent to the pulpit do not stay because of pressures both internal and external with which they cannot or do not wish to cope. To add fuel to this fire, the contemporary church member expects to know that the pastor is honest and trust worthy, and that his/her word means something and can be relied upon. Church members will bring their own "issues" and biases and lay them at the feet of the Prophet and expect that the Prophet will speak to those issues, solve the problem or at least have some clear view of the path ahead. To say or do less leads to inescapable distrust of the Prophet.

Third, fear and prophetic pain. I write now of something that is so intensely personal that I wish I could avoid it all together. Every thoughtful preacher/prophet will wrestle between two questions: Am I doing enough? Am I doing too much? The answer is, YES! Pastor, Priest or Prophet, you will never escape the internal pull that has you running to meet the latest need, grasping for the ringing phone, or trying to save someone else while not losing yourself in the process.

You want to know what makes the Prophet bleed? It's the empty seat for Sunday worship. It's the blank stare in the pews all because of the sermon they did not understand. It's the child that left home that the parents cannot find. It's the senseless overdose where the church should have intervened. It's the fear of letting the world know the real you and the overwhelming need to be transparent for the benefit of those before whom you stand. And if, perchance, you do not bleed at these teaching moments of your ministry, it may be time for some psychological assessment of your fitness for the demands of this work.

Ultimately it is our fear that produces our pain, and in our pain we bleed. We bleed for those around us. We bleed because of those who rule over us. We bleed for ourselves. Your task and mine is to take the urgent needs of church and community and to wear them as a loose garment, while at the same time you approach them with urgency, passion, and a determination to be an Ambassador for the King.

Prophet? Yes! Preacher? Yes; But you will preach while you bleed. You are human, you are frail and you will be challenged. But if you read the end of the Book you will discover that we win!

Take Heart from the Lessons of the Thorn Bird

First, every Thorn Bird has a song to sing. Perhaps only one song but that bird could sing more sweetly than any other.

Second, every Thorn Bird was aware of his destiny. The Thorn Bird is not suicidal in pursuit of its thorn, but confident that the same God that created him and taught him how to sing was the same God that would teach him how to die.

Third, the Thorn Bird does not rest until he finds the tree to which he is destined and then...

Fourth, he rises above his own agony! And God smiles ... for the best is only bought at the price of great pain. Is there a preacher in the house?

There is a high price to be paid for the privilege of preaching. It is the "price of great pain." We who stand Sunday by Sunday at the intersection of pulpit and pew do so knowing full well that we are not what we intended to be; we are not what we were designed to be; and that which we represent somehow falls short of who we really are. That is why we come to the closing lines of these writings on preaching with a word that is both searing and searching, a word that is designed to explore and expose the existential reality of preachers and their preaching.

There is also, without question, a problem we face when it comes to the matter of preacher integrity; a problem when it comes to the matter of living up to the expectations God has for my life and yours; a problem when it comes to the matter of just being authentically who we say we are.

And, to come rather quickly to the crux of this matter, it has become difficult for me, it has become difficult for us, to fulfill our task in the preaching ministry because we are so caught up in this quagmire of spiritual neediness, personal deception, external hurt, and internal pain.

I remember the days of my ministry with the Antioch Church of Houston, Texas. She was formally Mrs. Dotson but those of us who knew her best called her Mother Elsie. I had not taken charge of this pastorate very long before Mother Elsie came to my office with a bit of pastoral counsel she was certain I needed. These were her words: "Pastor, don't let these people kill you!" Startled, I accepted her counsel graciously as I was sure she was sincere. I really didn't understand her meaning. Did she literally suggest that I was in danger, in harm's way? I went about my work with diligence and energy but I hid my fear and kept it internally secret.

Seasons now have changed and the zeal and headiness of my more youthful years have come and gone. Mother Elsie is gone now but I think I now understand. Whether we are preachers or prophets we all stand vulnerable and open before the world. Like you, Dear Reader, we are all cut from the same cloth. We all react swiftly to unkind words; we are all subject to fits of depression and self-doubt. We are all frail, shaped in dust, frail creatures of the moment. We are all human. The "S" on your chest is a dangerous illusion. You are not protected from "kryptonite." Thank God for the Mother Elsies of our ministry. Our congregations see, hear, and intuit far more than we think. Listen well. No matter how long or how well we have been engaged in this calling, from time to time even when we preach, we bleed.

When properly understood, authentic religion is intended to be serious business. Tragically, however, while religion is serious, too often it appears that there are few among us who take it seriously.

There are other factors which must be central to our discussion of authentic religion. Our religion is inauthentic whenever we do not approach it with deference. We are on the wrong path when we believe that the church is the building on the corner. Our internal GPS has misdirected us when we believe that the church is just another organization and not an organism, designed by God to bring life to the body and hope to the world! We will never be the church God intended us to be as long as we concentrate on finance and fail to live in faith. We have misinterpreted scripture whenever we choose to believe that the pastor is just another man, or just another woman, rather than one who has been anointed, set apart, filled with the Holy Ghost and born again.

Consider the *Thorn Bird*. While the *Thorn Bird* is impaled while singing, she is at the same time attached to a thorn of inescapable death. Like the Thorn Bird, we who preach do so with an inescapable agony - we cannot evade it, we cannot avoid it. While we are called to preach to others, more often than not we are preaching to ourselves. Our task is to acknowledge our sickness and our pain in the nearly impossible task of becoming, in the words of Henri J. M. Nouwen, "wounded healers." It was Nouwen's task to call those who preach to acknowledge their own suffering and to make that acknowledgement the starting point for ministerial service. More to the point, it was Nouwen who insisted that

> *"the great illusion of leadership is to think that man can be lead out of the desert by others who have never been there."*[37]

There is, to be sure, an unseen but deadly process of internal bleeding that places the church and our ministry at risk. It is, I believe, the reality toward which Dietrich Bonhoeffer, a German Lutheran pastor, theologian and anti-Nazi dissident, pointed us to with this chilling reality: **"When Christ calls a man He bids him come and die."** And, truth be told, we are literally preaching while bleeding.

This preaching business is not at all what I thought. When first I stood to preach I thought preaching was little more than the use of flowing and flowery oratory from the public platform. I thought preachers were blessed to wear designer garments and drive fancy cars. I thought all preachers had to do was to preach "feel good" sermons, and to preach a prosperity gospel in spite of the hell in which people lived. I thought the goal of every preacher was to find that special "sweetness" in his or her throat and then to "whoop" "until

---

[37] Henri J.M. Nouwen, The Wounded Healer: Ministry in Contemporary Society. Published November 1, 1994 by Darton, Longman & Todd (first published 1979)

the power of the Lord come down"—while the people were caught up in shouting, spiritual dancing or speaking in tongues, an ecstatic frenzy for which there appeared to be not one rhyme or reason to justify such histrionic behavior.

On the other hand, someone should have told me what this preaching business is really all about. Someone should have told me that too often to preach is to be desperately lonely and to have no genuine friends upon whom you can trust and rely.

Someone should have told me that to preach is to proclaim a word that no one really wants to hear, based on a book no one wants to live by.

Someone should have told me that to preach is to be afflicted with the stammering tongue of Moses, or to stand like Jacob at the ford of some Jabbok River—spent from wrestling all night with the angel of God and now living with a limp. You may be sent to an as yet undesignated destination with Abraham and Sarah to the crest of Mount Moriah, or be sentenced to stand on some Sinai there to watch bushes burn that are not consumed, and lead people on a forced march around Jericho's walls until the walls come tumblin' down.

Someone should have told me that in some midnight hour my sleep would be disturbed like Samuel's and that there would really be no choice in this matter; the only response one can make to that midnight summons is: "Speak Lord, thy servant heareth."

Someone should have warned me that I would try to book passage on a ship bound for Tarshish caught in a storm over in Joppa, then be sent home in the entrails of a great fish or at least that, like Ezekiel, I would be required to pastor a congregation that had caskets for pews, skeletons for pall bearers, no organ for anthems, no choir to sing, no deacons to pray, and no souls to shout.

Someone should have told me that, like John the Baptist, my preacher status would qualify me to have my head separated from my shoulders and presented to some Herod on a silver platter by a dancing Herodias, or like Peter and John I would spend my time down at the temple called "Beautiful" preaching to beggars with no silver and no gold to my name, paying no attention to the fact that all the man asked for was "change;" or, like John the Revelator, I would be left to preach to rocks somewhere on an isle called Patmos on the Aegean Sea, somewhere with hands "scarred and sore" and bleeding from cutting up rocks. Someone should have told me that if you preach you will bleed.

Yet, my story is more than marginal notations found in an ancient script. This pain is real. I say again, no one told me.

No one told me how disrespected and defeated I would feel that Sunday when those women held up the funny paper to read while I tried to preach.

No one told me how to react that night when the trustees refused to give me a $30 a month raise.

No one told me how I would only learn to preach after the undertaker around the corner gave me suits dead men were to wear for casket repose but were redirected and re-purposed for me to wear while preaching.

No one told me what kind of preacher I would become when the parsonage in which I lived was just two doors from the local house of prostitution.

No one told me what text to preach when bodily threats came against my life and I dressed for preaching in a bullet proof vest.

I did not understand why, Sunday after Sunday, it felt as though I was preaching the Gospel in a graveyard and no matter how careful I tried to be it always seemed as though I had blood on my hands.

Somehow, I could not reconcile the joy I was supposed to know, or the faith with which I was supposed to preach, with the hell I was going through. Week by week I did not understand the men and women who beat a path to my door in search of counsel, looking to me for answers, and the bereaved looking for consolation; when, if the truth be known, I was the one in need of counsel. I was the one whose life was nothing but broken shards of glass. I was the one with a broken heart. I was the one in desperate need of compassion and consolation. I was the one on life-support in my own private intensive care. I was the one hemorrhaging from internal hurt. I didn't know it then but I was literally preaching while bleeding.

Further still, there are significant causes for our bleeding. When, like Karl Barth, we approach the pulpit and our preaching with the Bible in one hand and the newspaper in the other, our bleeding is always in direct proportion to the bleeding of the people in the pews we serve. Do not fail to understand many of us are called to preach in communities where the shedding of blood is a continuous flow.

When we consider the life and death struggles of Black men with representatives of law enforcement, our children slaughtered in the streets, tail-light stops that turn into suicide ropes, and unarmed teenagers shot in the back while fleeing for their lives, who's bleeding?

Why is it that in the twenty-first century we are still wrestling with issues of race and bigotry and the not so subtle tensions that accompany those issues? Who's bleeding?

The State of South Carolina has taken down its Confederate flag, yet there remains the reality of a presidential election that threatens to create a far deeper level of power based on privilege and race, that threatens to take this nation back to its shameful beginnings of bigotry, racial discrimination, and hate. Who's bleeding?

Has it become apparent that the African American church is no longer the prophetic voice that speaks with trumpet tones for those who seek racial justice and economic equality? We claim to be the sons of Issachar but do we really have "an (adequate) understanding of the times" and do we really "know what Israel ought to do?" Who's bleeding?

Have we come to the point where the words of violence and oppression are indelibly etched on the bodies of African Americans to such an extent that our systemic dehumanization is taken for granted. The question becomes: do Black lives matter?

Is the blood of our generation washed over the steeples under which we worship to such an extent that the church is no longer able to provide leadership to our communities, or show the path to justice for the people we are sent to lead? Our children are hungry and need to be fed. Our cities are polluted with lead infused waters. The neglect of our schools as well as the neglect and miseducation of our children is, at best, criminal. This new generation of Millennials and all the rest have neither confidence nor hope that the church or her preachers have the capacity to bring about the change we need. Who's bleeding?"

Black Lives Matter

Black Lives Matter. These three words, when heard, summon a visceral reaction among persons at all levels of the political spectrum. These words were joined together in response to what seemed to be a rash of police shootings of men and women for seemingly no reason other than the fact their skin was Black. The skin was the sin.

According to mappingpoliceviolence.org,

- Police killed at least 104 unarmed Black people in 2015, nearly twice each week.

- Nearly 1 in 3 Black people killed by police in 2015 were identified as unarmed, though the actual number is likely higher due to underreporting

- 36% of unarmed people killed by police were Black in 2015 despite Black people being only 13% of the U. S. population.

- Unarmed Black people were killed at 5x the rate of unarmed whites in 2015

"Only 13 of the 104 cases in 2015 where an unarmed Black person was killed by police resulted in officer(s) being charged with a crime. Four of these cases have ended in a mistrial or charges against the officer(s) being dropped and four cases are still awaiting trial or have a trial underway. Only four cases (Matthew Ajibade, Eric Harris, Paterson Brown Jr., and William Chapman) have resulted in convictions of officers involved, with a fifth case (Walter Scott) resulting in the officer pleading guilty."[38]

And the beat goes on. Beyond this census report or any other, the reality is that the number of Blacks that are being killed by police is disproportionate to the

---

38 Source: mappingpoliceviolence. org. US Census 2014

number of Black residents of the United States. That is what has caused the problem. Writing on the issues raised by the Black Lives Matter movement, Dr. Michael Eric Dyson adds this to the conversation:

> *Black frustration mounts when Blacks have what they think is clear evidence of police misconduct, and the failure to appreciate Black life is reinforced when there is a rejection of what stands as proof that their lives do not matter the same way as white lives. They cannot matter the same way because they cannot be seen the same way ...the images from real life cameras fail to convince whites of what Blacks see: that Black lives do not matter as much."*

Black people are joined together in what Dyson has tagged "a fellowship of fear." Dyson reminds us that Martin Luther King, Jr., in the wake of the Watts riots, said that **"a riot is the language of the unheard."** When you come upon those who are critical of the Black Lives Matter movement you must simultaneously remember that "Blacks are profiled, abused, dismissed, disbelieved, set aside—literally killed and un-mattered. Black people know what it means to feel insecure in one's home, unprotected by one's government; no space is safe or adequate to prevent the plague of assault just because one is Black."

It should be no oversight that prompts us to remember that women are directly affected by this national epidemic of Black death. We amplify here the "voices of the unjustly aggrieved, symbolized in the important work of Kimberle Crenshaw, Columbia law professor and co-author with Andrea J. Ritchie of the report *Say Her Name: Resisting Police Brutality Against Black Women.* The *Say Her Name* protests in 2015 in several cities across America were fashioned by activists to highlight the countless Black women who have been harassed, harmed, and even murdered by the police.

There are obvious implications which flow from these important movements. What we have not begun to realize is that in these United States of America, **"things could get worse before they get better."**

If you think that in this country Black lives don't matter, things could get worse. Do you think Black men are unjustly targeted and profiled by the police and that such abuse will end overnight?

Do you see that in this country, despite the goodwill of more than a majority of this nation, racism is rising, bigotry is out of control, and with the election of Donald Trump to the Presidency of the United States of America, there appears to be no end in sight?

Do you think that in this country the only thing we need to worry about is Donald Trump? Have we forgotten that the water is still polluted in Flint? Don't look now, things could get worse. Help us God!

And things **will** get worse unless and until we get up, dust ourselves off and get back in the race. I believe God has placed Black people at this pivotal point of social history, a dramatic watershed of human history, to determine once and for all if we will be serious change agents or be content to return meekly to the hellish plantations of our slavery.

It could be that Donald Trump is no more than a pawn used by God to wake Black people from their slumber. We can no longer excuse ourselves because we contend with some that the Civil Rights movement is dead or irrelevant, or that we are too tired to struggle or too slow and apathetic to run the race. Donald Trump is there for one purpose and one purpose only: to expose how sick this nation is!

In my analysis, **Black Lives Matter** has two parameters. First, **what I think** and, second, **what I think really matters.**

What I think is that the whole state of affairs within our communities is a reflection of the very judgment of God. From the days of our labor on the soil of Southern plantations, the Black Church and the Black preacher have been front and center in the fight for justice and equality. The Black Church was always the meeting ground for the movement, whether in a slave shanty in Louisiana or in Brown's Chapel in Selma. The Black Preacher was always cloaked with the mantle of leadership, whether an unrefined Harriet Tubman (a preaching woman with a man's name—Moses!) or Martin King from Morehouse. Yet when Travon Martin was gunned down in Florida, or when Freddie Gray lost his life in a police van, or when Sandra Bland was found dead in her cell, what major, visible, audible role did the church play in leadership for this crisis in our community? In all of this, who was our Medgar, who was our Malcolm, who was our Martin? Whose picture goes up on the funeral home fan this year? Or has the Black Church really become so irrelevant that we have lost our right to lead? What do I think? What I think is "where there is no vision, the people perish."

What I think is that if we no longer have leadership status within the African American community, that may be the reason violence has engulfed our cities from Minnesota to Baton Rouge. One of the primary functions of the Civil Rights movement of the 60s was to keep before our people the life-preserving, society saving process of non-violence.

News Flash. Black people are not non-violent by nature. The counter-culture would have you believe that Black people are all by nature docile and mild-mannered. No, we were taught to be non-violent on the Edmund Pettus Bridge, non-violent on the back roads of Mississippi, non-violent on that treacherous strip of highway known as U. S. Highway 80, non-violent with James Meredith walking through troops at Ol' Miss, non-violent with Rosa Parks seated on a Birmingham bus, non-violent when nine Black students broke through the color barrier at Little Rock's Central High. Who forgot to teach non-violence?

We didn't forget, we're just tired. Tired of being stepped on, tired of being stopped for broken taillights and then losing our lives, tired of being shot at and being unable to shoot back, tired of taking a switch-blade to a gun fight, tired of being treated as though we are not important, we are not necessary, and we do not matter. I believe we may have come to that time when we need to pull out that book by William Henry Grier and Price Cobbs, **Black Rage.** This was a book written in 1968 and the argument of these psychologists was that because Black people live in a racist, white supremacist social order they have necessarily been psychologically damaged by their environment which could account for black on white as well as white on black crime, a disposition to acts of violence no matter what the cost in terms of human life. Maybe now nearly fifty years later this volume may be a necessary tool to help us understand what appears to be a sense of necessity for killing as well as the necessity to bear arms in the first place. I fear we are literally driving each other mad!

I do not intend to imply here that there is room or justification for violence on either side of this issue. Still, think about it! How long did America think that Black people would continue the practice of remaining silent while serving as target practice for the police or for white men pretending to "stand their ground?" Something has to give. Change must come. The breach must be repaired.

So you ask again what we must think about Black Lives Matter? **Here's what matters:**

- What matters is that we define our protest not as what we say but what we do. There is a difference between shouted rhetoric and collective responsibility.

- What matters is how well we protect our homes and our families in our communities.

- What matters is how soon we learn to stop shooting each other, and abusing each other, and destroying our homes, and burying our babies in cemeteries before they reach puberty.

What matters is how well we train our children and teach them to value life, to value themselves and keep them safe.

This is what I think really matters:

- What really matters is how we become advocates for change and raise our voices to affect a systemic restructuring of an uneven and unfair criminal justice system; advocates that will hold Republicans and Democrats, Independents and Libertarians accountable for the change we seek.

- What really matters is how we express our faith in our public life. For example: What matters is how we use our holy edifices for sanctuaries as they have been historically used. In a time when whole cities are under attack for being sanctuaries for the "tired, the poor, the huddled masses yearning to breathe free" these monuments of our faith (our churches) that have been used historically to save us should now be used to give aid and comfort to others who knock on the doors for help. We, pulpit and pew, must tangibly demonstrate the salvation we preach.

- What really matters is how vocal we become to insist to the nation that the Voting Rights Act is not only restored but improved. And then we must go to the polls and vote. The election of Donald Trump to the presidency is the only proof we need to see the importance of the voting franchise.

- What really matters is how loud and how long we are able to protest until we restore sanity to this country and be-rid ourselves of this incessant romance with guns—until every officer of the law (black and white) who kills an innocent person is sent to jail where they belong. And if not we shall all find ourselves preaching as we bleed, and perishing together as fools. What matters is how we insist that the Church of the Living

God return to its prophetic pulpit and preach till "justice rolls down like waters and righteousness like a mighty stream."

Come back to Elijah:

Follow, if you will, and let me tell Elijah's story. When it comes to preaching while bleeding, as we have seen in the previous chapter, no one fills the subject as does the Prophet Elijah, the Tishbite, who was of the inhabitants of Gilead. But what we know of Elijah is that his assignment was to stand before a King named Ahab and prophesy.

> "Ahab, as the Lord God of Israel lives, before whom I stand, there shall not be dew nor rain these ears but according to my word."

Surely you remember that the only test of an authentic prophet was that his prophecy came true and was fulfilled. Such was the case with Elijah; his prophecy came true. Not long after the drought had overtaken the prophet's land, his brook dried up. Then came ravens with room service to feed the prophet night and day. There was that encounter with that widow woman down in a little out of the way town called Zarephath. All she could do was to bring the prophet a little water in a vessel and a morsel of bread in her hand.

If that were not enough, then the widow woman's son died and Elijah had to stretch out his body over the child three times; looks like the Prophet had resurrection power in him; death was suspended that day and the widow's son lived.

And then that contest on Carmel. You remember how Elijah preached:

> "How long halt you between two opinions?
> If the Lord be God, follow him: but if Baal
> then follow him!"

That's when something happened to the preacher. After all he had been through, Elijah is now in the wilderness. Elijah's brook has dried up. Ahab and Jezebel have 450 prophets of Baal with whom Elijah would have to deal. And there sits Rev. Elijah, under a juniper tree, eating biscuits and drinking water, thinking about the things that really matter, wondering whether or not *he* mattered. The Reverend Dr. Elijah: Broken. Bi-polar. Depressed. Miserable. Melancholy. Suicidal. Prepared to die. He is bleeding through his preaching.

If this is the case, then perhaps we should all be called Elijah. Let me tell you what the statistics say. In a survey conducted by *Focus on the Family* and the Fuller Seminary, their research revealed the following:

- Fifteen hundred pastors leave the ministry each month due to moral failure, spiritual burnout, or contention in their churches.

- 50% of pastors' marriages will end in divorce.

- 80% of pastors feel unqualified and discouraged in their role as pastor.

- 50% of pastors are so discouraged that they would leave the ministry if they could, but have no other way of making a living.

- 80% of seminary and Bible School graduates who enter the ministry will leave the ministry within the first five years.

- 70% of pastors constantly fight depression.

- 70% said the only time they spend studying the Word is when they are preparing their sermon.

The hardest thing about these numbers is that they only tell half the story. The other half is that congregations don't know or understand the nature of pastoral stress. And when a pastor breaks down or has a moral failure, congregations, for lack of a better word, "kick the pastor to the curb."

"Most statistics say that 60% to 80% of those who enter the ministry will not be in it 10 years later, and only a fraction will stay in it as lifetime career. Many pastors, over 90%, start off with a true call and the enthusiasm and the endurance of faith to make it; but something happens to derail their train of passion and love for the call."[39]

And yet, that's where you and I are—divorced, burned out, depressed, and kicked to the curb. But, come Sunday, we've got to preach. That's where you and I are—filled with anguish, struggling with anger, often alienated from ourselves and from those closest to us. But, come Sunday, we've got to preach.

And the problem is, we can't tell anyone! No one would believe it if we told them. When they see us on Sunday we're all dressed up. We've got our hair combed and our shoes shined. We're wearing a designer suit complete with silk tie and Gucci shoes. We roll up to church in a BMW. Nobody wants to hear our troubles. Most folk don't come to church to hear the preacher complain. Most folk would really prefer that we suffer in silence ... so

> "Don't tell me your troubles;
> I've got troubles of my own."

After all, we are the preachers. We are the prophets. We are the men and women of God. We are the newly minted, self-ordained Bishops. We live in that cloistered ivory tower called the Church. We live twelve feet above contradiction. But something is very wrong. We are really preaching while bleeding.

---

[39] R. J. Krejcir, Ph.D. Francis A. Schaeffer *Institute of Church Leadership Development*

What makes you bleed, preacher? You don't like Jeremiah; ask Isaiah! I asked the Prophet Isaiah about it and this is what Isaiah said:

> "Hear O heavens, and give ear, O Earth:
> for the Lord has spoken, I have nourished and
> brought up children, and they have rebelled
> against me. The ox knows his owner,
> and the ass his master's crib: but Israel does
> not know, My people do not consider."
> 1:2F.

What's the problem, Isaiah?

My problem is not with me; my problem is with my children. I need heaven to hear this; I need every prophet on the planet to understand what I'm dealing with. That which causes my difficulty is not external, it is internal. You must understand that this matter of preaching while bleeding is not a minor matter.

I do not claim to be a physician but I do know that the most dangerous blood loss is not the loss you are able to see but the bleeding that occurs that you cannot see. This internal bleeding of which I speak may be experienced in the tissues, or in the organs, or in the cavities of the body. Internal bleeding occurs when blood escapes the circulatory system and the life of the body is thereby endangered.

That which causes my pain is that which is closest to me. That which threatens me and places my life in jeopardy are those who have been with me night and day.

I don't have any trouble from the folk who live across town,

I don't have any difficulty from the church down the street.

I don't have a hard time with the alcoholics and the drug addicts on the corner. The ones you've got to watch are the ones you thought were on your side.

No, the ones I have trouble with are my children.

I brought them in this world; I was there when they sucked their first breath; I was there when they took their first steps, but they are the ones that give me grief. My children.

When they could not feed themselves, when they had no clothes on their backs, when they had no roof over their heads, I fed them and I clothed them. I built houses for them and still they won't do right. And now they want to talk back, to "sass" me!

The ones that cause me pain in church meetings, the ones I taught in Bible study, the preachers I licensed and the deacons I ordained, they are the ones that won't behave.

Think about it. The ones that I gave milk to drink, the ones I made a way for, the ones that I paid the tuition for, the ones that are driving the car I gave them and who are burning up the gas I put in their tank with my credit card, they are the ones that have rebelled against me!

The ones who never knew what a school was until I took them, they are the ones who are now educated, and sophisticated, and erudite; now they're so smart, they know more than I do; they have degrees and robes and gowns. That's why they now think they can rebel against me. That's what makes my preaching bleed.

Quite obviously, there's something wrong with my children. My children seem to have no interest in this thing we call the Church. According to my children, to be an atheist is now the latest fashion; to be agnostic is to be *en vogue*.

Read it again. My children have abandoned the Bible and, more to the point, there is in this generation a sense of rejection and persecution for those who dare to claim the name of a barefoot Palestinian Rabbi, hung amongst criminals on Calvary's rugged tree.

And it makes no sense. Go out in the barnyard, says Isaiah. There's an ox out there. Even a dumb ox has sense enough to know his owner. But Israel doesn't know. And not only that, there's a jackass out there. Even a jackass knows who puts the corn in his crib. But Israel does not know. Israel hasn't figured out yet who it is that puts butter on the bread. Israel doesn't know who makes a way out of no way. It looks as though Israel is not interested and not acquainted with the God who bears the government on His shoulders. So ...

I would preach if those who filled the pews were interested in hearing that voice crying in the wilderness.

I would preach if those to whom I preached had a clue about the One who made *"crooked places straight and rough places plain."*

I would preach if only my children wanted to know "*that the everlasting God, the Lord, the Creator of the ends of the Earth, faints not, neither is weary ...There is no searching of His understanding.*" But my children have rebelled against me. And that's why I'm out here preaching while bleeding.

Ah, but here's the problem. The reason I am preaching while bleeding is not because I am depressed. It is not because I have so many problems I can't tell anybody, or because I am burned out, or because I am suicidal, or because my children have betrayed me. My case, your case, our case may be the same as Jeremiah's. "I was deceived." And the only reason you could deceive me is because you are stronger than I am. I preached what you told me to preach. But the result of it all is this: You have deceived me.

The reason I am bleeding while preaching is because of a kind of divine deception. I write here today of the **unfairness of God**. It is this God who does not operate in the arena of Eternal equity. Every preacher who is a preacher sooner or later will stand in Jeremiah's shoes and offer up a complaint against the conspiracy of God. "Lord, you have deceived me and I was deceived."

And this is the strange irony of the matter:

> He who calls me to preach His Word
> is the same One who condemns me to suffer
> because of His Word. I was deceived.

> The One who made me preach
> is the same One who called me when I was
> unqualified, too young and too immature to
> preach. Here I thought I was somebody but in
> fact I was a nobody. I was deceived.
>
> The One who has insisted that I preach
> crippled me with a tongue that stutters and
> stammers, a tongue incapable of articulate
> speech. I was deceived.
>
> I hear people talking about Black Lives Matter,
> or White Lives Matter. I'm a preacher! I matter! `

How unfair of God. God set me up. It was a set-up from the get-up. God is responsible for this ecclesiastical, homiletic quagmire in which I find myself. God is the Divine Culprit, the priestly perpetrator that has chained me to the pulpit and tethered me to the church. I was minding my own business when God conspired against me.

God told me He had arranged things before I was formed in the belly.

God told me that I had already been ordained and sanctified in my mother's womb.

God told me that my ministry would be GLOBAL. God told me I would be more than another "store front" preacher. God said I would be "a prophet unto the nations."

God told me that I should not be afraid of their faces,
God put God's hand on my mouth,
God put God's words in my mouth.

God gave me an agenda, God gave me a vision for ministry to *"root out, and to pull pluck down, and to destroy and to throw down, to build and to plant."*

And here's what I got for my trouble: The folk are laughing at me. Every day I am held in derision. The whole town is laughing at me. And not only that, I can't get rid of it. It makes no sense but I can't get rid of this preaching thing. The more I preach, the more they laugh. Even when I say I will not mention Him, I will not speak His name any more; no more Sunday sermons for me, no more revivals for me, no more conferences for me. I'm done. I've had it. You can have it. I quit. I resign. I'm out of here!

But then it occurs to me that I *still* have a problem. I have a nagging, I have a persistent, hanging-on problem that will not go away. I've got this "fire" problem. It's in my belly. I've got this fire shut up in my bones and I'm tired of this holding it, and hiding it, and concealing it kind of problem. We might as well confess we feel the fire burning. And yes, we are still preaching but we're preaching while bleeding.

Yet there is something and some One that gives me strength to go on. There is something that gives me hope, even in a hopeless situation. And this is it. I have discovered that my bleeding is in relationship to the bleeding of the Christ I serve.

When we preach, simultaneously we bleed.

When we bleed there is a model, there is a paradigm for our bleeding.

When we bleed we do not bleed alone.

When we bleed we acknowledge that there is someone who bled before us that makes our bleeding make sense.

We do not bleed alone. We all bleed in our own way; in our own time and space. We do not bear these burdens alone. We are not in this struggle by ourselves. In fact, when we look back upon the history of God, when we look back upon the biography of God, when we look back upon the theological understanding of who God is and what God does, they call Him the ***"Suffering Servant."***

He who came to live also came to die.

He who is the rejected is also the redeemer

He is not impressive, He is not majestic, He is only a "root in dry ground."

He is despised and yet He delivers.

He is rejected and yet He reconciles.

His pain is my punishment.

He is "a man of sorrows ... acquainted with grief," and yet He wipes tears from your eyes.

> *"Surely He hath bone our griefs and*
> *carried our sorrows ...*
> *He was wounded for our transgressions,*
> *He was bruised for our iniquities,*
> *the chastisement of our peace was upon Him,*
> *and with His stripes we are healed."*
> ISAIAH 53:4F

"What this gospel teaches us to preach is not of thorns but of a crown. After all, it was Jesus who "took it all, paid it all and changed it all.... He changes hurt to healing. He changes the poison of sin into a medicine of grace. He changes the crown of thorns to that crown of life which He has and which He gives to all who love Him." [40]

But what shall we do with our bleeding? If there were anyone who could be accused of preaching while bleeding it was that tent maker from Tarsus. Paul went to great lengths in the writing of his books to expose the autobiography of his pain. Listen to Paul's record:

> *Of the Jews I received forty stripes save one.*
> *Thrice was I beaten with rods. Once I was stoned,*
> *thrice I suffered shipwreck.*
> *A night and a day I have been in the deep.*

It was the Apostle Paul who spoke of a man he knew. He does not give his name; he only says, *"I knew a man."* Looking back on his history he says that for fourteen years this man he knew had a condition. But there was something about this man, like that Thorn Bird, who was given a thorn in his flesh.

Said Paul, *"...lest I should be exalted above measure through the abundance of the revelations, there was given to me a thorn in the flesh."* This appears to be the work of Satan but I just had a thorn in my flesh. I do not know, says Paul, if this turned out to be an out-of-body experience or not but I do know this - there was a thorn in

---

40 Taylor, Gardner, "How Shall They Preach?" Progressive Baptist Publishing House, Elgin, IL, 1977, p. 116.

my flesh. I was among the walking wounded. After all, I was a student of Gamaliel,

> "I was circumcised on the eighth day, the stock Israel, of the tribe of Benjamin, an Hebrew of the Hebrews, as touching the law, blameless."

But after all of that was said and done, "there was given to me a thorn in the flesh." I didn't deserve it. I was preaching but I was bleeding. Three times I asked the Lord to remove this thorn from my flesh. Three times, over and over, and over again, I asked the Lord to take this pain away and set me free. But that's when I heard him say: "MY GRACE IS SUFFICIENT FOR THEE: FOR MY STRENGTH IS MADE PERFECT IN WEAKNESS."

What shall I do with our thorns? We must preach, but we must not ignore our thorn. This is what Paul said:

> "I keep under my body, and bring it unto subjection, lest by any means when I have preached to others, I myself should be a castaway."
> I COR. 9:27

We are preaching while bleeding yet there are two things of which we are certain and sure:

> "I am not ashamed of the Gospel of Christ, for it is the power of God unto salvation to everyone that believeth."
> ROMANS 1:16

> "I reckon that the sufferings of this present time
> are not worthy to be compared with
> the glory which shall be revealed in us."
> ROMANS 8:18

And, remember that Thorn Bird? In the moment of its birth, it is in search of a tree with the sharpest of thorns. The thorn of which the legend speaks is a thorn that promises to permit that bird to rise above its agony and take the bird from life unto death. It is still clear to me that the best of life is only bought at the price of great pain. That puts me in a different place and I am called to remember one of the favorite injunctions of Dr. Gardner Taylor. ***"When it comes to the matter of preaching, no matter where one begins, make haste as quickly as you can, cross-country to Calvary!"***

I know Someone that came into this world in search of a tree. I know some One who entered this life purposefully and intentionally in search of a tree. I know SomeOne who came into this world in search of a tree and in search of nails like thorns. "On a hill far away stood an old rugged cross, the emblem of suffering and shame."

I know SomeOne who preached while bleeding. The record is they beat Him all night long. But He kept on preaching.

They placed a crown of thorns on His sacred head but He kept on preaching.

They nailed Him hand and feet but He kept on preaching.

They pierced Him in the side but He kept on preaching.

The blood came streaming down but He kept on preaching.

> *Alas and did my Saviour bleed*
> *and did my Sovereign die?*
> *Would He devote that sacred head*
> *for such a worm as I?*
>
> *Was it for crimes that I have done*
> *He groaned upon the tree?*
> *Amazing pity, grace unknown*
> *and love beyond degree.*
>
> *Well might the sun in darkness hide*
> *And shut his glories in,*
> *When Christ, the mighty Maker died,*
> *For man the creature's sin.*
>
> *But drops of grief can ne'er repay*
> *The debt of love I owe:*
> *Here, Lord, I give myself away*
> *'Tis all that I can do.*

Doxology

I've been reading the newspaper again. Dangerous habit. At the writing of these words, the New Year has yet to complete its first-month cycle, and the impossible has already occurred. The Congress has passed economic legislation it did not bother to read—a cruel plot to keep the poor poor and the rich rich. Somewhere through the hours of the night, Obamacare was all but given a death sentence along with the millions of Americans who saw their hope for consistent healthcare vanish with the frigid temperatures of the night. The struggle for a meaningful immigration policy is on the edge of destruction by leadership that would rather build walls than colleges.

What kind of leader is it that prefers to kill dreams rather than support those who dare to dream? Now by an intentional slip of the tongue, the President of the United States has described the nations of Haiti and Africa as "s~~thole nations," a harmful, hurtful use of language that only further divides a nation in search of itself and a President in search of his soul.

And what do I hear from the leaders of this nation who have the capacity to effect change?

"We've got to do better."

Sounds to me like the same old sound bites we give to the press.

"This is not who we are."

Sounds like the same old sermon we've been preaching all along.

"Wait till mid-term elections, we got to give our President a chance."

No. We've heard enough of that.

Such sermons are not the stuff of critical change. We live in what Martin King called "the fierce urgency of now." The time is now to stand up, show up and speak up.

We must stand up, so the world will know we are not asleep.

We must show up, so the nations of the earth will know our word is our bond and that we are not a "Ship of Fools" heading into some foggy black, eerie, scary cover of night. We must speak up. We are not a Ship of Fools carefully arranging seats on the Titanic, nor were we ever intended to be a Ship of Fools sailing along with a dysfunctional crew and a deaf captain who is also **just a little blind!**

The time for solitary leadership invested in one person, or in one politician or his political party is dead and gone. We all must be preachers. We must all be prophets. Doing better is not enough. The margin of error is too great. "Better is the enemy of Best. Better is the enemy of perfection."[41]

What we seek is to be **"one nation, under God, indivisible, with liberty and justice for all."** Anything less is unacceptable. Anything less invites immorality. Anything less is breathing room for tyranny. Anything less brings shovels to the nation's graveyard where we shall forever bury the truth in preference to "fake news." Anything less seals the fate of the nation to the resurgence of hatred, fear, racism, sexism, bigotry, misogyny, and at worst, a gagging and galling ignorance in leadership at the highest level. It promotes anew authoritarian impulses that can be the undoing of our democracy, our government, and our way of life.

Yet the unassailable truth is this: Mr. Trump is not the issue. The issue is America. The issue is wheth-

---

[41] *The Enemy of Good is Better* by Michael Salcman, Orchises Press, 2011

er we shall continue to be consistent with the principles of that faith that has brought us safe thus far. The president is not the issue. The issue is how swiftly and responsibly men and women of good intent, with the purpose of patriots, will stand erect in the face of such arrogance. The president is not the issue. Should we be able, by some strange coincidence of time and circumstance, to compel his resignation and clear the White House of every Secretary down to the last paper clip and unplug every computer and every phone and cast them in the Potomac River, Donald Trump will still have a job and Air Force One will still be waiting to take him to where ever he needs to go for his next political rally or to play his next round of golf.

That is why we so desperately need a prophet. A prophet who, with skill and compassion, can help us come to grips with who we are and how we came to this point in our collective history. We need a prophet who is able and willing to come to the city square to argue effectively for the people before whom he stands. We really do need a prophetic leader who will be able to give voice to the people as he becomes the spokesman for a new generation, many of whom have yet to be introduced to the Source of our faith. We need a preacher who can stand at the center of the city and yet have "street creds" of authenticity as he/she walks the streets. We need a leader who has the heart of a shepherd with the anointment of a preacher. The only criteria are that they come to the pulpit, as Jeremiah would have it, with a word from the Lord!

And you might be the one!
"Truth forever on the scaffold."[42]

You might be one our times demand!
"Wrong forever on the throne."[43]

"Yet that scaffold sways the future and beyond the dim unknown

Standeth God within that scaffold
Keeping watch above His own!"[44]

Is there a prophet in the house?

---

[42] Excerpt from "Beams of Heaven as I Go" written and composed by Charles Albert Tindley, The United Methodist Hymnal Number 524
[43] Ibid
[44] Ibid

. 6 .

A Passion for Preaching

A *Passion for Preaching*

> *"I wouldn't give a nickel for a religion
> I couldn't enjoy."*

That's a direct quote from my father, H. Beecher Hicks, Sr. And he meant that thing. My father loved to preach. It excited him. It was the thing that literally made him jump out of bed every morning. Because he loved to preach those who heard him found his approach in the pulpit both effective and infective. I shall never be the preacher my father was.

Perhaps that's the point of it all. Authentic preaching ought to be infectious; someone should "catch" something. Through all our preaching someone should catch the faith, catch the hope, catch the healing, catch the salvation, catch the fire, catch the grace, and catch the love. If the preacher is not in the "infection" business the church will never grow, the ministry will not thrive, the preacher will not survive. If the preacher is not "infected" the preacher will not be effective. To speak in contemporary jargon, the gospel needs to go "viral," the church must catch a virus until the whole world gets it! I need to get it. You need to get it. We all need to get it. It is only in the infectious nature of Spirit-filled preaching that its impact will spread "from heart to heart and breast to breast!"

How does the novice preacher or even the elder statesman come upon this infectious gift? After all, we are given gifts with differing abilities and capacities. We are not the same; we were intended to have different assignments with differing abilities and capacities. The Scriptures say quite clearly that some shall be "hewers of wood while others will be drawers of water." Yet, whether preacher or prophet there is a need for passion in our preaching.

While thinking this matter through I came to a strange observation, if not a revelation. Barack Obama is a preacher. He is a preacher, though not in the sense of a licensed, ordained, professional clergy. If preaching may be defined as one who from time to time gives moral or religious advice, who is an inspired and chosen spokesman with the ability to communicate the oracles of God, speak to the existential position in which people find themselves, and demonstrate in his being the grace and love of God, I suspect that Mr. Obama, licensed or not, is as much preacher as any of the rest of us. At the risk of redundancy ...

> **OBAMA? THE PREACHER? REALLY??**
>
> As an aside, if Mr. Obama is not a preacher he is certainly illustrative of those who are not of the ordained ministry, those who have not enrolled in the local seminary, and will never be called 'Pastor' that it is possible to have and to exercise a prophetic gift even though you don't hang a "Reverend" hat on it, and certainly not 'Prophet.' He does become, however a role model of the manner by which persons may be prophetic even if they stand outside of or over against what we know as authentic "church." The evaluation of ones ministry life pursuit is not a measurement of how we say what we say; it's not what you say, it's what you do.

In point of fact, however, you have only to review his preaching record—the words of parental/pastoral (?) compassion for the parents of slain children at the Sandy Hook Elementary School, the soaring yet inspirational oratory on the rusted iron supports and struts of the old Edmond Pettus Bridge in Selma, Alabama, and certainly his "sermon," complete with a sidebar solo of "Amazing Grace" at the funeral for the nine victims at Mother Emmanuel AME in Charleston, South Carolina—and you are forced to reach the conclusion that the man can preach! So much so that most of his addresses to large crowds concludes with a serious call and response that is typical of the African American Church and its worship. It is clear that Mr. President has spent time in somebody's church and has absorbed well its preaching lessons. Perhaps Jeremiah Wright?

Listen carefully and you will hear from him the broad but unmistakable outline of the sermon he has prepared, the careful use of scriptures to tie and strengthen the outline structure of the oration, the poetry with which he has constructed every paragraph, the unwitting invitation to **"call and response"** which is typical in the African American church's oral tradition, and surely the skillful manner by which he leads the audience/congregation to a "close," typically a high-energy, raised decibels of voice, repetitive ending of inspiration, added to the audience-raising, hand-clapping, Rest-On-Your-Feet! ending of the sermon. He probably would not agree with the preacher designation, but it's the truth anyhow!

Early on in his rise to recognition and ultimately to the presidency, President Obama frequently used the phrase "the fierce urgency of now." This phrase, of course, was not original with the President. Writing in his book, *Beyond Vietnam: A Time to Break Silence*, Dr. Martin Luther King, Jr., suggested, as delivered in April 1967 in the Riverside Church of New York City,

> *"We are now faced with the fact, my friends,*
> *that tomorrow is today. We are confronted with*
> *the fierce urgency of now ..."*

It is always in the light of urgency that the preacher/prophet is called to stand and to speak. On its face, surrendered to the hand of the preacher is a book we call the Bible, tattered and worn by some, ignored and unread by others, and yet there is an urgent requirement to read its lines and to live by its precepts.

So, this is where I'll hang my hermeneutic hat. The first obligation of those who would be either preacher or prophet is to listen to other preachers (with or without portfolio). Listen carefully to hear their outline, anticipate their destination, learn from their gift, appreciate their usage of language, the eloquence or the elegance, or the crudity of expression and the impact that either will have upon the audience. You can only learn what you already know if you are only listening to yourself.

The second obligation is to preach with an unmistakable urgency and intensity. This, of course, has nothing to do with speed or haste. Those two imposters can pronounce a death sentence on your sermon. Intensity may be conveyed through the raising of an eyebrow; urgency may be seen by slowing down, giving a moment for some crucial point to sink in and be absorbed.

The urgency of my preaching necessarily comes from the context of the community before me. There is an urgency of life and death proportions that marks those who sit on Sunday seats. They come to church because there are urgent issues with which they must contend in their daily lives. They need to know that you take their lives seriously. The congregation will quickly detect that there is a special something in you that touches that special something in them. Consequently, the congregation will take your sermon seriously if you do.

To discuss the purpose of preaching is to be concerned about its meaning, its objective, and its desired aim and goal. That is the WHY of preaching. What the young homiletical student wants to know is by what formula, what prescription, what methodology the preacher achieves his or her aim.

That's what I learned from my students. Not the WHAT, not the WHY, but the HOW of preaching. They want to learn how to preach in 1-2-3 / A-B-C order. They want desperately to understand the mechanics of preaching. Not the theoretical; the intensely direct, practical, down to earth, and "doable" methodology they can use long after the teacher has gone home. Well, let's see ...!

First. How do you do what you do?

Honestly, it's difficult to say, primarily because every sermon requires its own process. One can approach the matter of preaching a text head-on or by using a more nuanced method. The method that is best is the one that works for you and lets you work within the parameters of your gift, ability, and comfort.

Second. OK, then, what is first thing that you do? And what is the source of your ideas?

That's a better question. My first assignment is to remain open and watchful. I am open to see and understand the events and circumstances that surround me. I want to see what God is doing and saying in my community. I am initially not so much interested in finding a text as I am hopeful that a text will find me.

Sermonic ideas can surface from numerous sources: Current events, news articles on TV/newspapers, magazines. Conversations with a neighbor across the back fence. A comment overheard while standing at the bus stop. Wherever people are, God is. God has an inexhaustible catalogue of sermon ideas. I've even been known to carve out a sermon from movie titles, "Rap" or other forms of popular music. Just listen.

Third. I see. So when a text has found you, what's your next step?

At that point I am ready to listen to the text. I read the text in various translations and versions. I do my exegetical work and scout out the meaning of words and concepts that may be foreign or forgotten. Words have meaning and how we use those words have consequences. Following on, I surrender the matter to prayer and wait.

Fourth. For what are you waiting?

I am waiting for God to speak. I am waiting for God to give release not only to preach the sermon but to preach it in a way that would be consistent with God's will for God's people to hear. If the text has found me, then God is obligated to fill my mind and my mouth with the words God would have me speak.

Fifth. What do you do if God doesn't speak and you still have to preach?

> *"I waited for the Lord and he inclined unto me and heard my cry!"*
> (PSALM 40:1)

Waiting to hear the speaking voice of God may be the most difficult part of this process. Continue to wait; God will speak if you are acquainted with God's voice.

More to the point, not only am I waiting for God to speak, I am waiting for God to "call." The "Call" is not a singular act of God. God's call must be repeated time and time again. There is a tragedy for those who have no sense of Call. William Augustus Jones speaks of it in this manner:

> *"God puts it plainly, 'I have not sent these prophets, yet they ran; I have not spoken to them, yet they prophesied.' That's the problem, says the Lord—prophets without portfolio, unofficial operators, ambassadors*

Who have not the King's blessing, uncommissioned communicators ...
Unregistered runners, unsanctioned sprinters, uncertified couriers,
...phony proclaimers, sham servants, bogus brokers, uncommissioned, unchosen, uncalled." 45

Sixth. What's really important to you?

Thanks for asking. When it comes to sermon preparation and delivery there are at least three things that are important to me. First, what I think. It is important that I am not so rushed to prepare a sermon that I fail to give the matter adequate thought. It is important that I have exercised myself extensively mentally so that I have taken advantage of the resources of the mind. I must think with mind and heart for they will both be reflected and revealed with each word that I speak.

The second thing that is important to me is what I hear. God speaks in so many languages, images, media, and voices that it is critical that my ears are tuned to the Eternal. It is important because the thing of value is not what I am saying but whether I am hearing the voice of God through the voices and languages of the people.

Strangely, both my thought and my hearing are very often caught up in the process of prayer and the

---

45   Jones, William Augustus, "Responsible Preaching," Aaron Press, p. 41, 1989

discipline of sitting still. Sitting still is one of the most difficult of disciplines and perhaps the most productive. God never speaks in confusion; only in that God-consecrated stillness is God able to gain your attention and has the room to speak. Prayer before one begins, prayer while one reads, while one thinks, while one writes. The whole process must be surrounded, grounded, and under-pinned with prayer. When it comes to preaching, "Little prayer, little power. Some prayer, some power. Much prayer, much power." "Be still and know..." Your choice.

Seventh. You've been preaching for a long time and we notice that you are a manuscript preacher. Is that the best method to use?

There is no "best" method. The best method for preaching is the one that God has given to you and then surrendered back to God. Some are liberated to preach with only a brief outline that can be reviewed ahead of time and then set aside to be open and dependent on the leadership and guidance of the Holy Spirit.

> *"I Believe I'll Testify ..."*
>
> "One concrete lesson we learn from Gardner C. Taylor is that internalizing the manuscript can lead to homiletical freedom within the established framework of what one has planned, and

> can produce more meaningful connection with one's listeners...(He) made changes in order to remain connected to his congregation,"
>
> JARED E. ALCANTARA,
> Homiletics in conversation with Gardner C. Taylor
> Crossover Preaching, p. 243

Others may choose to be exclusively extemporaneous with only a few key points memorized and some order that facilitates memory and then rests on the articulate gifts of the preacher. I have watched many a preacher come to the pulpit with a manuscript in hand, review it briefly while waiting, and then leave the sermon in his seat. Dr. Charles Booth is an excellent example of this gift. This is a true gift from God.

Impromptu has to do with that preaching which occurs when one is called upon to preach without prior notice and without opportunity for extensive preparation. In that case the old-time adage applies. *"Every preacher should always keep a sermon in his head and a sermon in her pocket!"*

Written sermons are my personal preference. There are several reasons. Once again, writing gives the preacher the opportunity to engage the mind fully. Words have meaning and impact not only through what the preacher says but what the congregation hears. There is no such thing as a "perfect" sermon; writing, however, gives one the opportunity to choose the right word, select the appropriate phrase or rearrange the way the argument of the sermon is presented. Writing is your memory's safe guard.

It is certainly true that God has promised to bring all things to your remembrance but when your memory is on "overload" and your cell phone "mailbox" is full, it's mighty fine to know that you can go to "file" and find it in black and white. Your writing skill, when developed over time can bring power and elegance to your spoken work. Remember, you don't know it all and you don't have to remember it all. Memory, outlines, extemporaneous—none of them will exempt you from the prayer, study, and hard work required. Writing does not exempt one either; the challenge is to find what is on the paper, surrender it to the Holy Spirit and then tack it, like wall paper, on the broken heart of some sinner who sits before you.

Eighth. What about alliteration?

Use carefully. Alliterative phrases are attractive to the tongue and delightful to the ear. This use of words has the capacity to attract the attention of the hearers and paint word pictures in the mind. When used sparingly they can be an awesome tool; when used to excess they can detract from the purpose of the sermon. Alliteration falls into the category of creativity. Creativity is certainly a gift. Its use however can be overdone and one can be accused of going over the top, of being "too cute by half." Beware creativity gone amuck.

Succinctly, Dr. Maurice Watson of the Metropolitan Church in Largo, Maryland advises, *"The sermon should be a wedding between creative homiletics and hermeneutical accuracy."* Narrative preaching, expository preaching, first person preaching, and many other forms of communication can be creatively used to propel the Gospel. At any case, all preaching must be disciplined, creative, accurate, and undergirded by prayer. No matter what methodology is used for preaching, it is critical that the preacher is thoroughly absorbed and saturated in his or her message; the weekly coming of the Holy Spirit is no antidote for the ill-prepared or the ill-informed.

Ninth. What is it that makes you passionate about your preaching?

That's easy. I'm still learning how to do it. After fifty-seven years, preaching is a gift I yet do not know how to handle; it is a challenge I have yet to master. Every time I stand to preach I know I'm going to be surprised by God. Sunday by Sunday, year by year, God has kept God's promise: "And I, if I be lifted up from the earth will draw all men (women) unto me." I learn every time I open my Bible and attempt to preach I am forced to remember that it's all in His Hand. He just permits me, from time to time, to take up space in His center pulpit chair—but it's always His chair and not mine; but the real work belongs to Him and to the Holy Spirit. The Holy Spirit alone adds power to the gift. To God be the glory. Years ago while sitting with Dr. William August Jones in the Bethany pulpit the time for me to preach had come. Dr. Jones leaned over to quiet my nerves and say to me: "Expect a Miracle!" And I did!

What makes me move? What makes me passionate? Over the years of my ministry I have discovered that the strongest and most accurate source of my passion has come from the persons I have been privileged to serve as "Pastor." What a sweet word! Through the expanse of these years four congregations have generously called me Pastor. Such generosity has been a benediction on my life. They are the ones, Second Baptist in Mumford, New York; Mount Ararat Baptist in Pittsburgh, Pennsylvania; Antioch Missionary Baptist Church of Christ in Houston, Texas; and dearest to my heart, Metropolitan Baptist in Washington, D.C. and Largo, Maryland, who have taught me lessons in preaching, given counsel whether I wanted it or not, forgiven me, loved me, and provided for me and for my family. In fact, I must tell you, they have showered me with their love, far more than I deserved.

My preaching has been punctuated by the pain as well as the smiles I have seen on their faces. My struggle to preach was always greeted with tolerant understanding, almost an embarrassment of grace. My attempts at homiletic creativity have been met with uncommon charity. It is one thing to be called Preacher, quite another to be called Prophet.

I don't think prophets go to cemeteries to lay the faithful to rest; nor do they make sick calls to hospitals where pain and sickness reside. Pastors do.

I don't think preachers spend much time counseling wide-eyed newlyweds or blessing howling babies. But Pastors do.

You have never preached in your life until you stand and look out on the faces of those who call you Pastor. That's the thing that gives power to my prayers, urgency to my preaching, joy in my heart, and a shout in my soul.

Tenth. Any final comments?

Yes. Relax. Don't obsess. God's got you! Do what you do, do it as God has instructed and enjoy the ride. If you do what you enjoy, you will never work a day in your life! God grant that on this day you shall come to know the source and the reality of this peculiar passion and strange grace that permits you to Preach While Bleeding!

. 7 .

A Question for Preachers

Are you Serious?

When the southern sun comes up in Arkansas, nothing moves. There is no wind, not even a whisper. There is no movement in the pine trees that stand like soldiers along the road. Even the skeeters don't move; too lazy to fly and bite. Fields lie fallow, deserted, dry. Cotton picked and weighed. The living is *not* easy. The fish are not jumpin'. Poverty is palpable. For too many, hunger is too real. Too many houses are really no more than shot-gun shacks you can look straight through from the screen door in the front to the screen door hanging on the back. This is truly the place where time and heat, oppressive heat stand still.

But it's Sunday morning, time to go to church. There is nothing more important on this day than going to church and being on time. Dinner was cooked yesterday. You know, religious folk don't work on Sundays; that's the Lord's Day, the Sabbath. So they always cook Sunday's dinner on Saturday. The rolls covered with a towel, the collard greens on low heat to make sure they are tender when called on. The only thing that is not ready is the chicken; but it will be ready, along with the corn-on-the-cob, when they get home from church. Papa will catch a chicken or two in the backyard and wring its neck on its way to make a contribution to that huge pile of fried chicken that appears on the supper table every Sunday the Lord sends.

The year is 1961, the place is Pine Bluff, Arkansas where the economy is non-existent. The largest employer is a toss-up between the local paper mill which lends its stifling aromas to every afternoon breeze or a little African American College known as AM&N, now the University of Arkansas at Pine Bluff. Of course, the economy of the struggling college was truncated by racists circumscriptions inflicted on it by the Arkansas legislature.

But today is Sunday. The family is on the way, through the heat, walking through the Arkansas dust. When they arrive they are reminded that this is one of the Sundays the Pastor is at the "other" church. After all, the church cannot afford a 4-Sunday preacher;

they'll just have to get another preacher to fill in because of the Pastor's absence.

A knock at my dormitory door disturbs my late morning sleep. A classmate knocks again and tells me that I have a call on the payphone at the end of the hall. I arrive at the phone in a fog and begin to listen to a stranger's voice on the other end of the line.

"Is this Mr. Hicks. Mr. Beecher Hicks?"

"It is. Who's calling? How may I help you?"

"This is Deacon Jones of the Fifth Street Baptist Church. (fictional church name) I am calling because we need a preacher tomorrow morning.

"Tomorrow?" "Morning?"

"Yes, Sir. We got word that you were one of a number of preachers on the campus that might be able to help us out when our Pastor is away. You are licensed to preach aren't you? Can you help us?"

"Yes, I am licensed. What time tomorrow morning?"

"Eleven o'clock. As always. By the way, what is your fee? We usually get an offering between $5 and $10."

"I will be grateful for anything you do. See you in the morning."

And so began my journey in ministry, my journey in the profession called "preaching." It was my first "preaching engagement" and I really didn't know what to do. I had no one locally upon whom I could call for advice. Was this a step too soon? Should I accept an honorarium? Really? Oh, and by the way, what am I going to preach? What shall I say to these people I do not know. The only sermon file is the one I have in the one suit coat pocket that I own, and that's just a few sheets of paper with some scattered notes. This was destined to be a preaching disaster of the first magnitude.

The more I began to think about it the more I became excited by the challenge. The ink on my License to preach, still wet and not yet on my wall, was signed by my father and authorized by the only church I knew, Mt. Olivet Baptist in Columbus, Ohio.

Somehow, in my mind, I could not minimize the importance of this initial preaching opportunity. I had proclaimed my "call." It was now up to me to demonstrate it. This would be the first testament to my faith. This would be the first Sunday when someone in the real world would look me in the eye, and upon that examination determine if my preaching was at all authentic, if at all serious.

I remember that day's dawning. I remember making my way, walking through the heat, to my first assignment. I have absolutely no idea what I preached, how well I preached, how long I preached or if anyone joined church that morning, or even how many of the Saints of God in Pine Bluff were there in attendance. I only know that, by God's grace, I survived the ordeal and made it through the test. Thanks be to God.

By the way, the offering for the preacher that day was $5. Looks like they knew what it was worth! The one thing I learned, however, was this: Preaching is Serious Business. Take a look at **GENESIS 22:2-6.**

When properly understood authentic religion is intended to be serious business. Religion, as the expression of our faith, is intended to be a reflection not only of time-tested truths as revealed in Scriptures but also a reflection of the experiential evidence of one's personal walk with God.

Authentic religion is, by definition, more than a periodic testimony or the glib recital of worn expressions and clichés or even pious phrases borrowed from generations now gone. Quite to the contrary, authentic religion can only be verified through a personal traverse of mountains high and valleys low. To be sure, the Christian journey is tedious, its path fraught with dangers, enemies are present on every hand, the cost of discipleship is high and, if the record of history is correct, it may even cost your life. Again, when properly understood authentic religion is intended to be serious business. Tragically, however, while religion is serious too often it appears that there are few among us who take it seriously.

You will forgive what seems to be an overly aggressive cynicism. Strangely enough, however, my cynicism is born out in the crucibles and chronicles of that Gathering we call the Church. That is why it seems to me that we have learned the language of religion, and we have rehearsed the rituals of religion, but far too many do not really take it seriously.

We have learned how to pray, we have learned the jargon of prayer, we have rehearsed the prayers of our elders and our ancestors but rarely do we expect that our prayers will be heard in heaven or rise any higher than the ceiling. Somehow we do not take it seriously.

We have choreographed the worship—who moves when and who steps where and for how long. But no one knows whether God accepts or appreciates our worship because even God knows that sometimes we do not take it seriously. Or, maybe we do know:

> "When ye come to appear before me, who hath
> required this at your hand, to tread my courts?
> Bring no more vain oblations; incense is an
> abomination unto me; the new moons and Sabbaths,
> the calling of assemblies, I cannot away with it;
> it is iniquity, even the solemn meeting."
> (ISA. 1:12-13)

We have even taken the words of scripture, put those words to musical notes, enhanced those words by percussion and bass, enlivened those words with stringed instruments and organs, and then sung those words until it appears we have learned songs that even angels cannot sing. Still, regrettably, we do not live the life we sing about in our songs. We do not take it seriously.

I would not belabor this matter unnecessarily but when you consider the expressions of our religion in the twenty-first century, tell me, how serious is it? Really? ...

When there appears to be no litmus test to authenticate our testimony and no question ever asked to verify the claims we make,

How serious is it?

When by every measurement it appears that our witness is weak, our commitment is questionable, our work is half-hearted, our sacrifice is tepid, our offerings are unpredictable and our praise lukewarm,

How serious is it? ...

When those who fill our pews come with an insatiable hunger for the good news of the gospel and then leave the walls of the church still hungering and thirsting for a word that has upon it the imprimatur of the Eternal.

How serious is it? ...

When it seems we have even taken the blood from the cross, the "old rugged cross," an emblem of suffering and shame, and burnished it in brass to make it pretty and decorated it with gold to make it acceptable, with never a word about that chilling blood-saturated death God's Son suffered on that awful tree—How serious is it?

When the world looks at the church, examines the difference between what we say and what we do and when the world raises questions about the difference between our commitment and our claims, and when the secular culture decries the dichotomy between our behavior and our beliefs that is *precisely* the reason the question comes to you and to me, are you serious?

Of course, the question "Are you serious?" may be interpreted quite differently, depending upon the tonal inflections of voice by which it is carried:

To ask the question "Are you serious?" is, in the first instance, the question of incredulity. The question itself falls into the realm of 'I don't believe you.' The question is in the category of 'you gotta be kiddin!' The question places its accent on the third word: Are you *serious?* The question portends that somewhere along the line a grave error has been made, some great expectation insults the boundaries of logical thought. Some requirement is made which appears to be above and beyond the limitations of human reason and the only logical question to be asked in that circumstance is this: "Are you serious?"

Biblical examples abound which speak to the unreasonable requisites of religion.

Consider Jesus and His disciples. They were cut from common cloth; crude and unsophisticated. Jesus was from Nazareth, from somewhere on the other side of the tracks, living with his parents who were so poor they had neither "pot nor window"; and you know nothing good ever came out of Nazareth. Foxes had better holes than His; birds had better nests than He could offer. They functioned without coats and often without shoes. And yet He spoke to them one day on the issue of the incredible assignment to which they would give themselves. Said Jesus:

> "If any man will come after me,
> Let him deny himself,
> And take up his cross and follow me.
> For whosoever shall save his life shall lose it;
> And whosoever will lose his life for my sake
> shall find it."
> MATTHEW 16:24F.

To which the only reasonable reply of those disciples must have been: Are you Serious?

Or consider, if you will, those exiles in Babylon. They were the best and the brightest of Israel's population. They had witnessed the terrible destruction of their land and temple. Everything they valued had been taken from them; everything they loved was now lost.

And there they sat on the banks of the River of Babylon, exiles, captives, prisoner's in a strange and foreign land. But that's when someone said: it's time for choir rehearsal. We know you're in a difficult state, we know you're in "between a rock and a hard place," but this is what we want you to do: "sing us one of the songs of Zion."(Psalm 137) Sing us one of your church songs. Sing us one of your anthems. Sing us one of your foot-pattin' songs. To which came the reply: "How shall we sing the Lord's songs in a strange land?" In other words, "are you serious?"

Ah, but you must dig a bit deeper for the hidden meaning buried within this text. It is found in the twenty-second chapter of the first book of Moses that we commonly call Genesis. Of course, one will find these words as the concluding lines of a drama that had its beginnings in the Ur of the Chaldees. You will recall that it was there that God spoke to a man named Abraham, and then instructed him to leave his country and his kindred for a land that God himself would show him. You remember as well that Abraham was not alone; by his side was his wife of long years' duration—and he called her name Sarah.

Yet of the things that you remember most of Abraham perhaps it is his walk with God. Abraham was known as the "friend of God." It is said that Abraham and God communed together as a man communicates with his friend. It was always God and Abraham / Abraham and God. They had it like that! In fact, so well did they communicate that their friendship was marked by Covenant. The book of Genesis says it quite plainly:

> *And when Abraham was ninety years old and nine,*
> *The Lord appeared unto Abraham, and said unto him,*
> *I am the Almighty God; walk before me,*
> *and be thou perfect.*
>
> *And I will make my covenant between me and thee,*
> *And will multiply thee exceedingly...*
>
> *And I will establish my covenant between me and thee*
> *And thy seed after thee in their generations*
> *For an everlasting covenant, to be a God unto thee*
> *And to thy seed after thee.*
> 17:1FF.

You will recall, of course, that both Abraham and Sarah had exceeded their years of fertility and they dreamed no longer of the prospects of procreation. Abraham's seed had dried up and Sarah's womb had closed, never to be opened again. And yet, the covenant; and yet the promise:

> *And I will make my covenant between me and thee,*
> *And will multiply thee exceedingly.*

Abraham and Sarah had no nursery attached to their home in Canaan. They had no hope that Sarah would ever be fruitful. In fact, that's exactly why they got caught up in that Hagar/Ishmael scandal because it seemed that Sarah would never give birth. And yet the promise:

> *And I will **make my** covenant between me and thee,*
> *And will **multiply thee exceedingly.***

So incredible was the claim, so unlikely was the eventuality that Sarah would ever give birth that even when she heard the announcement of her impending pregnancy, the Bible says that both Sarah and Abraham laughed. And in response came the question: **"Is anything too hard for God?"** For there is yet the promise:

> *And I will make my covenant between me and thee,*
> *And will multiply thee exceedingly.*

And all of that is in chapter seventeen. By chapter seventeen - problem solved, baby delivered, case closed, game over. But five chapters later, if you leave chapter seventeen and make your way to chapter twenty-two, something so breathtaking is happening it strains the limits of logical faith.

By chapter seventeen everything is under control, the difficulty has been dealt with, there is no need to worry, there is no need to fret, Abraham and God are (BFF) best friends forever. But five chapters later the walls cave in, the roof collapses, the wheels come off, the rug is pulled, and the bottom falls out.

Only five chapters later it looks like God has forgotten all about Abraham, it appears that God cares nothing about Sarah and it looks like the promise is a thing of the past.

So now, Chapter 22. This is what it says:

> *And it came to pass after these things,*
> *that God did tempt Abraham, and said unto him,*
> *Abraham: and he said, Behold, here I am.*
>
> *And He said, Take now thy son, thine only son Isaac,*
> *Whom thou lovest, and get thee into the land of Moriah;' and offer him there for a burnt offering*
> *upon one of the mountains which I will tell thee of.*

There come those moments when what God requires of us causes us to even question God: *Are you serious?* I can hear Abraham now:

- You say you want me to go where; you say you want me to do what? Are you serious?
- You say you "called" me for what; you say you want me to preach what? Are you serious?

- You say I've got to walk through the valley of what and live in the shadow of whatever? Are you serious?

- You say that my lot will be angst and agony, sickness and suffering and, like Job, the day will come when I must take my place on the ash pile of my own pain. Are you serious?

- You say in order to make it to the Kingdom I must go through much tribulation. Are you serious?

- You say in order to rise I must fall; you say in order to lead I must follow; you say in order to be loved I must be hated; you say in order to get I must give; you say in order to achieve I must fail; you say in order to win I must lose; and you say in order to live I must die. Are you serious?

Ah, but you must come closer to this text. Abraham unwittingly raises for us the question of **the seriousness of God.** Abraham raises for us the question of the purpose of our pain. Abraham raises for us the specter of what even appears to be the capriciousness of God. It is the question that assumes that God requires of us the unthinkable, exposes us to the inconceivable, and demands of us the unachievable. To which our only response can be: **Are you serious?**

After all of these years Abraham and Sarah have been waiting and hoping, praying and preparing for the day when spermatic fluid would make sudden impact with receptive eggs and at long last a child would to them be born.

But now the most miraculous thing has occurred. Sarah is pregnant! Nine months' gestation have passed. Isaac slips down through the birth canal of history, there is celebration all around and then twelve years have come and gone. And that's when God says,

> "...Take now thy son, thine only son Isaac, whom thou lovest and get thee into the land of Moriah; and offer him there for a burnt offering."

God says, I know you love your Isaac.

I know your whole life is wrapped up in your Isaac.

I know your sun rises and sets in your Isaac; in fact, I gave you your Isaac, but **cremate him!** Turn your love into ashes.

Take him—take the one you love more than life itself—take him, put him on a pile of dry wood, slit his throat from ear to ear, and then set the wood and Isaac on fire as a burnt offering. And it is not written here. But the only thing Abraham could say, the only reasonable response that could fall from Abraham's lips, would simply be the question: **"Are you serious?"**

I need you to understand the Abraham dilemma. I offer the suggestion that when God told Abraham to walk Isaac up Mount Moriah and there place him on the altar as a burnt offering, Abraham didn't know what he was doing.

Please understand. Rarely will you see a jazz musician or a blues artist come to their instrument with music in their hands. Follow the beat of Gospel music and rarely will you see notes transcribed on paper. Ask B. B. King, or Ray Charles or Stevie Wonder: "**Show me your sheet music?**" They don't have any sheet music; they're just playing it by ear. Sometime God puts us in a situation where we don't know what we're doing, we don't know what we will encounter along the way, we don't know how things will work out in the end. Sometime the only faith we can muster is just to play it by ear.

There is Abraham walking up Mount Moriah, struggling with every step, uncertain what the end will be, plagued by questions and nagged by doubt. He doesn't know what in the world he will tell Sarah when he gets back home. He told her he was going to the mountain to worship. But now God has him on this mission that doesn't make any sense. He doesn't want to do it but he must. So he just plays it by ear.

I suspect there's someone here today that is faced with a problem they cannot solve. You don't know how you'll come out in the end so for right now you're playing it by ear. Nobody gave you the sheet music, nobody gave you the score, nobody gave you the notes by which to play the music of your life. You don't know if the chord is minor or major, you don't know the difference between a crescendo and a diminuendo, but somehow it's a song you've got to play. You even have a conductor's baton but you're not sure what to do with it. You cannot conduct the symphony of your own life; you certainly cannot conduct the life of another. So for right now, like Abraham, you're going through life's ups and downs but you're just playing it by ear.

I say again, the question, "Are you serious?" may be interpreted quite differently depending upon the tonal inflections of voice by which it is carried.

To ask the question "Are you serious?" is, in the first instance, **THE QUESTION OF INCREDULITY**. It is the question man asks of God. It is the question from the human side of the equation. I know I run the risk of redundancy but the question portends that somewhere along the line a grave error has been made, some great expectation is there which insults the boundaries of logical thought. Some requirement is made which appears to be above and beyond the limitations of human reason. Therefore, the only logical question to be asked in that circumstance is this: **"Are you serious?"**

But then God flips the script. For when the inflection of the question's voice is changed the impact of the question is dramatically and unalterably reversed. The question of **incredulity** is directed from man toward God but the question of *intention* is directed from God toward man.

On the one hand "are you **serious**" is a question which humans raise for God; but on the other hand, "are YOU serious," is a question which God raises for mankind. All this time you had a question for God but now God has a question for you. **Are YOU serious?**

The question here has to do with whether or not your religion is serious. Is there any substance to what you say you believe? Does your faith have feet or are you tied down to the traditions of yesterday? Slaves from their situation on plantation soil rang out the question: "Have you got good religion?" To which the response came back across cotton fields, "Certainly, Lord!" I thought I wouldn't have to ask this question. The question itself is this: is your religion serious?

- I know you have studied the church and have examined the church. But is your study enough or are you dealing in an archaic institution that, you must confess, is irrelevant at best and unnecessary at worst? And for all your theological inquiry and intellectual discourse have you been introduced personally to the God of your salvation? Is your religion serious?
- I know you know how to preach a Sunday morning sermon provided by the Lectionary but is there a sermon in your soul? Is there, like Jeremiah, a "word from the Lord," is there a fire "shut up in your

bones," is there a word you MUST preach that you cannot hold back? I want to know is your religion serious?

Sit up straight! Pay attention! There are only three ways that God knows if you're serious. And all three motifs of serious religion are resident in the text.

The first thing that God requires in order to know that your religion is serious is **ABSOLUTE SURRENDER.** It's in the text. Chapter 22, v. 2

> *Take now thy son, thine only son Isaac,*
> *Whom thou lovest,*
> *and get thee into the land of Moriah;'*
> *and offer him there for a burnt offering*

But that's not all. Chapter 22, v. 3.

> *"And Abraham rose up early in the morning..."*

That's all. "Take now thy son." (v. 2) "Abraham rose up." (v. 3)

No discussion. Take now thy son. Abraham rose up. No committee meeting. No meeting of the Board. Take now thy son. Abraham rose up.

There is no equivocation here. The surrender is absolute.

There will be no negotiation. The surrender is absolute.

Whatever it is, whatever God requires, whatever God demands, whatever the term and conditions, even if it means giving up the one I love with my whole heart, the surrender is absolute.

So, **you** want to know if your religion is serious but **God** wants to know what have you surrendered lately? If religion is serious something must be surrendered. The question of surrender is the question of importance; it is question of what matters? What is more important, the gift or the giver? God requires absolute surrender. What does that mean?

Self.	I surrender.
Position.	I surrender.
Pride.	I surrender.
Possessions.	I surrender.
Fortune.	I surrender.
Fame.	I surrender.
Talent.	I surrender.
All that I am.	I surrender.
All that I am not.	I surrender.
All that I shall be.	I surrender.
Whatever I'm holding on to.	I surrender.
Whatever is holding on to me.	I surrender.

> *All to Jesus I surrender*
> *All to Him I freely give.*
> *I will ever love and serve Him,*
> *In His presence daily live.*

But it's more than absolute surrender. If your religion is serious it must be marked by **ABSOLUTE SACRIFICE**. What God required of Abraham was nothing less than absolute sacrifice.

Here's the hard part: Before Isaac, Abraham had nothing. After Isaac, Abraham would have nothing.

"Abraham, take now thy son, thine only son Isaac, whom thou lovest." I will not take him from you; you must give him to me. I will not snatch him, I will not steal him, I will not kidnap him and, I promise you, I will not forsake him or desert him but you must give him to me. Whatever you have God will not take it from you; you must give it to Him.

Abraham did not know if he would ever see Isaac again. But an absolute sacrifice requires that you give it without any expectation that you will ever get it back.

I'm talking about absolute sacrifice.

We don't really want to talk about sacrifice.

We don't want to talk about feeding the hungry; we might get our hands dirty and that's too much sacrifice.

God does not require that which has no value; God requires that which is of the highest value.

Time Out! I need to be sure we're all on the same road. Dear Reader, I suspect that you would like to know in real world time just what I mean by sacrifice and then, what's faith got to do with it? When young persons do come to church they come with direct questions. As soon as they are seated all they hear is "give to this," pledge to that, 'Brother could you spare a dime,' could you write a check for the cause? If that's where you are, if that's where your head is, we need to start over.

The Abraham, Sarah, Isaac pericope has to do with at least five salient issues:

First, there is the Sarah situation. Why is it that the woman is always behind the door of the tent while the men sit in the living room to talk? When it comes to serious problems in the family, why is the wife always the last to know? If Abraham is the father of the faithful what shall we say about Sarah's faith? It is not simply that Sarah had faith in God; more to the point, God had faith in Sarah and trusted her to take the principal role in God's creative activity. When it made no sense, when gynecologist warned her of the risk and told Sarah she would never make it to term, Abraham trusted God but God trusted Sarah; from Sarah's womb would come the first in the long line of patriarchs. But when Sarah saw Abraham with the knife, the wood and the fire, what does Abraham tell her? He had to tell Sarah something. Something about faith?

Second, there is implicit in the Abraham, Sarah, Isaac pericope is the inescapable requirement for obedience. Obedience says "yes" when "no" is expected. Obedience says, "I'll trust Him" when reason says, "what God requires is more than I can handle." Obedience says, "I'll trust Him" when you must climb the rough side of the mountain all alone. Obedience says, "I'll trust Him" even when you can't track him and you can't trace Him, and you don't know what's just around the corner. And the truth of the text is simply this: where there is no obedience there can be no faith.

Third, faith is born on the winds of trial, trauma, and tribulation. What kind of faith will you have if all you have is sunshine and without shadows? Faith remains the substance of things hoped for and the evidence of things not seen. Many a Sunday service in the Black Church began its worship with saints who knew how to sing, "We've come this far by faith, leaning on the Lord." And yet faith is forged, not on the smooth side but on the rough side of the mountain.

Fourth, in order to receive what the Eternal plans for you, you must first leave where you are. You don't have to go back to your home but you can't stay here. You must leave the place of your comfort and go where God leads you.

Fifth, remember that Sarah and Abraham named the baby "Isaac" which being interpreted means "God laughs." Or, "He who laughs last, laughs best." Or, my translation, "when by faith you are obedient to God's word, you can smile."

I do not have the capacity to tell this generation or the next what will be required to restore that integrity of purpose with which the church began, to help the church live up to its Covenant, to make of it an institution that truly delivers what it promises.

When you survey the Abraham, Sarah, and Isaac situation remember that there is a difference between faith and sacrifice though they are cut from the same cloth.

- Faith and sacrifice are not equivalences though they live on the same street.

- Faith informs and deepens my relationship with the Eternal while sacrifice is my little way of praising the Name.
- Faith goes with me when I must climb high mountains; faith stands nearby to wipe the sweat from my brow and the tears from my eyes.
- Faith sits with me through long and lonely nights but my sacrifice is just my way of saying, "Thank You!"
- Faith stands with me in my battles and then brings my medicine in my room; and that's why every day of my life I have to give him a sacrifice of praise.

Maybe this will help you understand:

FAITH WITHOUT SACRIFICE IS POINTLESS; SACRIFICE WITHOUT FAITH IS DANGEROUS.

Reprise. When the world looks at the church, examines the difference between what we say and what we do and when the world raises questions about the difference between our commitment and our claims, and when the secular culture decries the dichotomy between our behavior and our beliefs that is precisely the reason the question comes to you and to me, are you serious?

The point I am making is that the church is not a perfect institution because Jesus left the church in clumsy, human hands. The church, however, has an imperative to continue in its work despite its feeble failings. Generations gone by now and I recall the way the church described its mission and purpose for being. They called it "The Old Ship of Zion." They said that ship had "landed many a thousand." I challenge all who are disappointed to harness that disappointment and bring to it the gift of your talents, your intellect, your curiosity, your adventuresome spirit, and your insatiable hunger for all things new and make the church what it is destined to be. You must only respond to my appeal if you are serious. It's not about money; God wants you.

God does not require that which is easy for you to give; God requires that which will hurt when you give it. Whenever you give the Lord absolute surrender, and whenever you give the Lord absolute sacrifice you can always expect that God will provide absolutely. Read a little further and you will discover that when Abraham placed Isaac on that altar, the wood beneath him, the fire in his hand and the knife to slit his throat, God sent word from heaven to an angel near-by Mount Moriah. In an instant, Word came from Heaven: *'Somebody stop him; he's serious!'* And they tell me that, right then and there, Abraham found his ram in the bush. He's serious. Send a ram in the bush. He's not playing religion; He's serious. Send a ram!

With the arrival of the Lamb, God kept God's promise. Think of it: God sent a Lamb! God sent a Lamb! To take away the sin of the World, God sent a Lamb. To walk upon this guilty sod, God sent a Lamb. To wash me in His precious blood, God sent a Lamb. I should have died but God sent a Lamb. I was so lost but God sent a Lamb. Right now I am found just because God sent His Lamb.

Don't you know the Lord will, yes He will, the Lord will provide. That's why they call Him Jehovah Jireh because the Lord will provide.

> *The Lord will make a way out of no way.*
> *The Lord will provide your every need.*
> *The Lord will open doors for you.*
> *The Lord will put food on your table.*
> *The Lord will prepare a table before you in the presence of your enemies.*
> *The Lord will anoint your head with oil and let your cup run over.*
> *The Lord will open the windows of heaven.*
> *The Lord will pour you out a blessing.*

The Lord will give you *"good measure, pressed down, shaken together and running over."*

Let me tell you how God will know when you're serious. It's not complicated; it's in the text. Chapter 22, v. 2.

> *. . . Take now thy son, thine only son Isaac,*
> *Whom thou lovest,*
> *and get thee into the land of Moriah;'*
> *and offer him there for a burnt offering*
> *upon one of the mountains which I will tell thee of*

But that's not all. Chapter 22, v. 3.

"And Abraham rose up early in the morning…"

When Abraham rose up that was the moment when Abraham said, "Yes!"

Religion is serious whenever you say, "Yes."

I preach for conversion today. I preach for salvation today.

Will you serve Him?
Will you surrender to Him?
Will you sacrifice what you love to Him.
Will you love Him?
Will you live for Him?
Will you praise Him?
Say YES!

Are You Serious?

When the north-eastern sun comes up in mid-January Manhattan, nothing moves but the wind. Whistling winds parade down Fifth Avenue, playfully running amid skyscrapers grand and tall. Taxi cabs line up at street corners waiting anxiously to rescue some poorly attired visitor to the City from the biting cold that only New York can offer. As the saying goes, something funny happened to me on the way to New York City.

I was a long way from Pine Bluff and its paper mill. I was a long way from the Fifth Baptist Church, and from St. Paul AME, and from AM&N College. To be exact it had been forty-seven years since those days of my beginnings. By now, I had completed my Master's degree in theology and soon defended my dissertation for the Doctor of Ministry degree from Colgate Rochester. I had pastored three churches and I was enjoying my fourth and final charge. God blessed our parsonage with three children and we soon learned to acknowledge that every blessing comes from the hands of a God who never fails to "open the windows of heaven."

And then, in 2011, history repeated itself. This time it was not a phone call; it was a letter. Now then, you must understand that when you are a student in seminary there are a limited number of subjects that are fit for discussion among them. You will always find seminarians discussing churches and/or their preachers. The name of one church frequently emerged from the conversations—The Riverside Church. As a seminarian I was confident that if there were a church that could be a foretaste of heaven it was surely Riverside in New York. Its long list of distinguished pastors, the largest church structure in the nation, and the 24th tallest in the world, outstanding social service programs and a pipe organ whose music was fit for the ears of God.

And on that day, I, of all people, had a letter—a personal letter, not mass-produced, a letter specifically intended for me.

> *Dear Dr. Hicks*
>
> *In the year 2010 and 2011 the Riverside Church will invite four preachers to be a part of our Distinguished Preacher Series. We would be pleased if you would consent to be one among the four preachers. Please ...*

Well, was I shocked or what? You're telling me that I am invited to preach where Harry Emerson Fosdick, and Norman Vincent Peale, and Ernest Campbell, and Robert McCracken, and William Sloane Coffin and Amy Butler and Brad Braxton, and James Forbes, preached? In that same pulpit? Are you serious?

My name is Henry Hicks, Jr., from Pine Bluff with the paper mill odor. Are you sure? I checked the addressee to be sure the letter had been delivered to the proper address. I had questions: was this a step too soon? Oh, by the way, what am I going to preach?

What shall I say to these people I do not know? Still, I could neither ignore nor minimize the importance of this step to stand and proclaim the Word of God in one of the great pulpits of the world. I had proclaimed my "call," I had washed thousands in baptismal waters, I had broken the bread and spilled the wine of blood and redemption and led countless persons to a life-changing commitment to Christ. It was now for me to carry that witness to a larger platform.

It was cold with flurries of light snow that January morning, wickedly cold on the day I would finally preach in the Riverside Church. I didn't want to make more of it than it was (I tried to remain calm, cool) but for me—**THIS WAS BIG!** I arrived alone; no Deacons to carry robes and Bibles. No friendly faces from Metropolitan to encourage me with their smiles and "amen's." No one was there except the One who had sent me, the One who had put His Word in my mouth and fire in my belly.

This would be a penultimate test of my faith. This would be the Sunday when someone from a world larger than any I had ever known, would look me in the eye, listen to my words, and examine my heart in those places where "deep calls unto deep," and determine upon that examination if my preaching was serious.

Think of these words not merely as another sermon but an opportunity for young preachers, old preachers, new seminarians and those barely able to take three credit hours each semester to continue in the struggle to be the best you can be through Christ.

The greater, ultimate test of my faith, will come when I meet my Savior face to face and His question of me will be: "Are you Serious?" Whether among my students, my parishioners, or those who follow from afar, God grant that when that day comes for you, dear reader, the world will know that you are, as I am, serious!

In Case I Didn't Tell You ...

Or, perhaps I should say, "there's more to life than preaching." To hear me tell it, the largest thing in life is to be able to preach. There is no height to which we can reach nor depth to which we can plumb that is not captured through this artful business we call Preaching. Not so. As with Hurricane Harvey, we swiftly are taught by the contrary winds of life, that the swollen creeks and bayous of our existence are swiftly filled to overflowing and all our lives are thrown into a death-dealing jeopardy.

Truth be told there is no one who loves to preach more than me. Preaching is a necessary component in the equation for the fulfillment of the Gospel of God. But there is more. There are times when we need not preach; we must prefer to listen. We need not always speak; we must find opportunities to learn. For some of those to whom we preach would be far better served by an encounter with small groups as together they learn to deal with their limiting beliefs and unhealthy behaviors. The preaching voice, the timbre and vibrato that some will need will come more through a whisper than through a shout.

The strength of our churches will be the efficacy of our efforts to combat substance abuse as well as to erase bigotry and racism and hatred from our landscape. The effectiveness and the impact of our ministry, the impact of the word we preach will not be measured by the length of our prophetic mantle but by the dusty difference our sandals will make on our journey to help someone survive. Our task as prophetic proclaimers is to find the revelatory key that will permit those whom we touch to have a genuine confrontation with the "self" prior to a confrontation with the Eternal. It is to permit what the Old Church called being "born again!" And the promise of God is surely this:

> *"If my people, which are called by my name,*
> *shall humble themselves and pray,*
> *and seek my face, and turn from their wicked*
> *ways; then will I hear from heaven, and will*
> *forgive their sin, and will heal their land."*
> II CHRONICLES 7:14

In case I didn't tell you, authentic prophesy and authentic preaching are not the consequence of a collar turned backward but of feet on a mission. Proclamation must never be judged by what it says but by the forward movement it occasions in the minds and hearts of the people of God. Far too much of our preaching, no matter how well-intentioned—is self-serving and is not illustrative of the authorities of the Gospel of Jesus Christ.

In case I didn't tell you, our preaching may only be defined by the willingness of the prophet to stand apart from personal restraints, a willingness to fight for the right as God gives us to see the right, and a determination to be the voice of leadership within our fractured and frustrated communities. Our preaching must give leadership to those difficult but necessary discussions that must be held regarding white privilege, white power, and race and grace.

In case I didn't tell you our task is to give a hand to those who are drowning in the flash floods of this world's hurricanes. The task is to speak life into the lives of those who are struggling foot-by-foot to make their way through the high waters of life. Those who suffer heartache, broken pieces and ruined lives are the ones we are called to claim and to rescue. Our task, as has never been before, is to unearth the truth of the past in light of the future we see in the distance. It is to that Great Commission we are claimed and called to go into the world, speaking light into darkness, healing into hurt, and power into pain. And as you go, as you preach, so shall you bleed. And that, my friends, is serious.

. 8 .

A Closing Word

No pastorate, no sermon, no ministry, has ever or will ever reach a level of human perfection. As humans, we are frail, vulnerable, stained by sin and, truth be told, most of us just spend our time upon the stage and come to the end wondering where the time went. Trust me, when it comes to human perfection I didn't even come close!

And yet, God has been good to me. Even through the writing of these words I am blessed. I have been blessed for 37 years to be the Pastor of a faithful and prayerful people. I have literally blessed them, married them, and buried them. I sought to be for them both priest and prophet, and to be sure, a loving Shepherd.

For the last few years I have been honored to serve as a teacher of preachers on the campus of one of the great theological seminaries of the nation. Think of it, my finger has been on the pulse of those who will guide the church and teach her people for coming generations. Whatever gifts God has given to me I now am privileged to pass those gifts along. I shall never be able to express my gratitude to the pastors of this community, across denominations, for their unfailing support. They have invited me to preach in their pulpits far more often than I have been able to reciprocate in kind. They have prayed with me in success and in failure. I shall be forever grateful for the strength I have gained through their support.

Now I am blessed to have shared the thoughts contained in the writing of this book with you and to know that these words shall travel and live far beyond the borders of my mortal life.

God has flooded my life with more than I could reasonably expect and with more challenges than I shall ever hope to master. In a manner of speaking, God has trusted me with "more."

More church, more praise, more civic responsibility, more friends, more adversaries, more assets, more liabilities, more opportunities to learn and to teach, more resources, more personal joy, a loving wife, brilliant children and grandchildren—God, for some unfathomable reason, has supplied me with more and literally honored me with opportunities to preach all over the world. What a mighty God we serve!

So, I thought I would add a codicil to this writing. This is a word to every church I have tried to Pastor, every preacher I have licensed or ordained, every board I have tried to lead, and to every group of students I have been honored to teach: My prayer to God is that God will grant you strength for your journey, hope for your tomorrow, the ability to bake a cake, and tall pillars to strengthen your faith and provide a spiritual base on which to stand.

My prayer is that God will provide for you enough storms so that you will learn of a certainty that He alone is Master of the Tempest, Sovereign of the Sea, and Captain of the Ship. My prayer is that God will open the windows of heaven and pour out blessing you don't have room enough to receive.

My prayer is that God will give you grace to handle life's thorns and that through perilous times you will be able to sing in spite of your pain.

My prayer is that God will equip you with an abundance of gifts so that whenever and wherever you stand there will be the inescapable presence of God in your throat as well as in your heart. My prayer is that every time you open the Bible your eyes will glaze over at the sight and sense of His magnificent Word.

My prayer is that God will give each of you such magnificent preaching gifts that every time you stand to preach or to witness, there will be such a fire in your belly it will literally burn you up. I pray that your preaching will have such fire producing power that you will become known as a Preaching Arsonist.

Try as I might there are lessons in homiletics that I could not teach. My prayer for you is that the Living Christ shall be your teacher and that the Holy Spirit shall guide you into all truth. My prayer above all is that God will give you grace, mercy, and peace but not just enough, I pray that God will give you more.

I suspect that at this sweet juncture of my life there is little energy for the writing of more books. There is energy, however to tell you how blessed I have been that God made each of you such a pivotal part of my life. There is enough energy to tell you that God has set our love apart and it shall remain a love that will not let us go.

The next few pages of this writing are the textual notes of my "Farewell Sermon" preached in the Metropolitan Church on the last Sunday of the year 2014. It is entitled *"And so I preached Jesus!"* Some have asked why I preached this sermon in just this manner? I have no reasonable response. I can only say, this is the Word God gave to me; in gratitude I give it now to you!

As for me, I'm out! But I'm not through just yet. My father was famous for talking about his end, the time to which he looked forward when he would bring to a close his earthly ministry. He always talked through the use of an illustration of a baseball game. My God, I can hear his voice now as he imitated and animated the closing of some game of memory. The players were all there: Jackie Robinson, Roy Campanella, Larry Doby, Don Newcomb, Say Hey, Willie Mays, and he seemed to know them all personally. And the whole congregation always got a kick out of hearing Jackie Robinson steal home from third base.

And yet as the people were on their feet rehearsing the sweet triumph yet again, there was a somber note that overtook him. He began to speak of the end. He could not stay with Mount Olivet forever but he knew with confident assurance that when his time on the pitcher's mound had come to an end, there would be another pitcher warming up in the Bull Pen!

There are other mountains to climb; more rivers to cross. I'll be with my grandfather, and my mother and my father, and we'll be off to save the world. Let there be no sadness here ... there's another pitcher in the Bull Pen!

"Hallelujah, Amen!"

> *"And I brethren, when I came to you, came not with excellency of speech or of wisdom, declaring unto you the testimony of God. For I determined not to know anything among you, save Jesus Christ, and him crucified. And I was with you in weakness, and in fear, and in much trembling. And my speech and my preaching was not with enticing words of man's wisdom, but in demonstration of the Spirit and of power."*
>
> II CORINTHIANS 2:1-4

And So, I Preached Jesus

Every preacher, claimed and called by God, will remember the day and the hour of the most disastrous sermon he ever preached. If it were written it is now a sermon buried deeply within the dusty files of his homiletic efforts, never to rise again in this world or in the next. If it were a text based on memory, or a sermon to be preached by impromptu gifts alone, surely every word would by now be "cast into a sea of forgetfulness" and, in similar manner, never again rise to see the light of day. And simply to add definition to the description, to preach a disastrous sermon is to preach and nothing happens. No "Amen's," no changed lives, no converted souls, no shouts of praise or echoes of Hallelujah! And it is true that every preacher will surely remember the most disastrous sermon he ever preached.

While I think on this matter, however, it is clear to me that most often the worst sermons that we preach may still feed some hungry soul while the best sermons we preach, in our estimation, most often falls short of the glory of the Gospel. We are, after all, Keepers of the mysteries of God, keepers of a sacred fire—a fire we cannot contain and dare not control. But the sum of it all is that for all of us who call ourselves preachers, this preaching is precarious business.

I share this brief note on the pain of preaching primarily because as I read Paul's first letter to his Corinthian congregation, Paul may be reflecting on his own experience of preaching. No doubt Paul had previously traveled to Greece and had visited there the city of Athens. Paul had come to know Athens, that great city of drama and culture. Largely known for its temples and monuments, Athens was a city greatly influenced by orators and philosophers such as Plato and Aristotle. And, no doubt, Paul had tried out his own brand of sermonic elocution and oratory there. They had permitted him to speak in the synagogue, don't you know, and in the market place and even in the Areopagus. But nothing happened.

Paul had displayed his oratorical gifts but nothing happened. Every Sabbath it was Paul's task to preach at the intersection of great minds and great ideas but when he tried to preach as the Athenians preached, nothing happened. Perspiration had broken out on his bald forehead but nothing happened. He had used his considerable intellectual acumen in order to compete with the Athenian scholars of the day but nothing happened. I say, it's a terrible thing when you preach and nothing happens. No changed lives, no converted souls, no shouts of praise or sounds of Hallelujah! Nothing happened.

But now Paul is at a different place in his preaching. Paul says it quite clearly: *"...When I came to you, (I) came not with excellency of speech nor of wisdom..."* Paul had made a discernable shift in his approach to his preaching. Paul had come to understand that **what** he was saying was more important than **how** he said it.

I hope you will permit this momentary aside but I need to tell you that young preachers just starting out on their pastoral journey tend to make mistakes in the homiletic structuring of their sermons. But this time Paul had learned his lesson.

The linkages are not clear. The comparisons are not precise. But when I came to Washington I had already preached some pretty disastrous sermons. I didn't come here trying to show off. There were some things I didn't know and did not know that I did not know. Thirty-seven years ago there were some lessons I had yet to learn. But I knew this. I knew God had sent me here. I knew God had ordained my ministry here. And I knew that I had only one assignment and that was to preach the glorious gospel of Jesus Christ.

So, says Paul, when I came to you I was not trying to be an orator. I was not trying to demonstrate my rhetorical skills. I learned the hard way what it was to preach a disastrous sermon. I could not compete with the intellectuals at Corinth. I was not trying to out think Plato or to surpass Socratic pedagogy. But across these years I've been with you. Across these years I've been with you in weakness, in fear, and in trembling. But there was no doubt in my mind just what I came to do:

> "...I determined not to know anything among you, save Jesus Christ, and him crucified."

Everything else had failed. Every word had fallen on deaf ears. Nobody understood a word I had to say. And so, I preached Jesus!

Every day Paul was forced to make an assessment of his assets and liabilities. The mirrors of his life told him that he was not a man handsome to look upon. He was short of stature. His head was bald. His nose was hooked. His eyebrows met in the center of his forehead. He had a hump in his back. And he walked with a limp, no doubt an orthopedic condition caused by falling from his horse while on his way to a Street called "Straight," or jumping over walls trying to escape from that hostile crowd in Damascus. That's why he walked with a limp and three times he asked the Lord to remove it but all God said was: *"My grace is sufficient for thee: For my strength is made perfect in weakness."* And so, I preached Jesus.

This preaching business is both precarious and painful. It is so on both accounts primarily because the thing upon which we were trained to rely is not available. We go to seminary to learn this business. We sit at the feet of learned scholars to learn this business. But what they're teaching we can't use. What they are promoting will do us no good. This is how Paul has it:

> *Where is the wise? Where is the scribe?*
> *Where is the disputer of this world? Hath not*
> *God made foolish the wisdom of this world?*
>
> *After all, says Paul "... the world by wisdom*
> *knew not God."*

I need to talk to somebody about **FOOLISHNESS!**

You cannot know God by how smart you are.

You cannot know God by how intellectually gifted you are.

You cannot know God by how many degrees hang on your wall.

You cannot know God by the velvet on your academic gown.

And the question is: WHY?

Why preach if the return is not equal to the investment?

Why preach if the world sees no value in the commodity you are selling?

Why preach if it is all dismissed as flash and mirrors, an "outside show to an unfriendly world?"

Why preach if in your popularity you gain the whole world and lose your soul?

Why preach if the ones to whom you preach are unimpressed with your sermon and fall to sleep before the text is taken?

Why preach if your sermons are so disastrous there are no changed lives, no converted souls, no shouts of praise or sounds of Hallelujah!?

And here's the strange thing. This is what the text says:

> "...It pleased God by the foolishness of preaching to save them that believe."

That's all you've got. Foolishness.

That's all you've got to work with. Foolishness.

All you have are what Dr. Gardner Taylor calls "clumsy tools." That's foolishness.

The world will laugh you to scorn all because they consider your work foolishness.

That's the metric by which your ministry will be measured. Foolishness.

And here's what I have discovered. Your sermons may prove to be disastrous. The world will listen to you and dismiss you as an intellectual lightweight. The world will think that both your oars are not in the water. The world will think the light's on but nobody's home. The world will think your elevator does not go to the top floor. But when they do, here's what you do, preach Jesus!

Paul said, "it pleased God."

If no one else gets excited, preaching excites God. It pleased God.

If preaching is frail and feeble still it pleases God.

If preaching is the only inadequate tool in your hands, it pleases God.

If no one else understands, He understands. It pleases God.

And that is why, no matter what else you may do; you may be preacher, servant or missionary, ultimately your task and my task is to preach Jesus.

I thought I needed to tell you this because this is a day when what the church needs, what the world needs is SERIOUS PREACHING. Do not misunderstand. I have no quarrel with my brothers and sisters who wrestle week by week to be faithful stewards of the gospel. But I do have a quarrel with those who have marginalized the craft we call preaching and in so doing have minimized the church.

The world no longer seeks moral guidance from the church because, as I read the newspaper, the church itself needs moral guidance. The world has set aside the moral authority of the church because we who have been commissioned to preach have chosen to be silent rather than to speak. "Rocks" are taking our place.

This is a day of apostasy—a day when the teachings of the church have been abandoned and the discipline of the church disregarded. Ours is a day of apostasy when the Bible has been dismissed and cast on library shelves as interesting but irrelevant fiction. Ours is a day of apostasy that literally means a *"falling away"* and the denial of the faith "once delivered to the saints." People will do anything in the church, and say anything in the church, and wear anything in the church, and cuss you out in church, and then dare the preacher or anyone else to say a word against it. Hear me today. The political leaders of this world will abandon the laws of God to gain favor with the latest political party, abandon the laws of God in order to make sin legal, abandon the laws of God to make wrong right and make right wrong.

This is a time for serious preaching. And serious preaching requires serious preachers. You know it's time for serious preaching when the Pontiff himself, the Pope of the Roman Catholic Church dares to accuse the church of an *"impotent silence,"* suggesting that the church and its leaders suffer not only from a *"lust for power"* but from what he calls *"spiritual Alzheimer's,"* which essentially means that the church has forgotten where it was trying to go or what it was here to do in the first place.

This is a time for serious preaching, I tell you. This is time when, in the words of Allan Boesak, God must raise up faithful men and women who have "heard God's voice in the cries of the oppressed, who (take) refuge in the love of God and from within that place of refuge (find) courage and step into the world to challenge the powers of evil." Not only must the church say something, the church must do something. In a day when serious preaching was needed, Paul, what did you preach? And so, I preached Jesus.

This is what Paul said: "For I determined not to know anything among you, save Jesus Christ..." In other words, there is a practical side to this preaching business. This is what Paul is saying: 'I don't know anything but Jesus. I don't teach anything but Jesus. I don't preach anything but Jesus.'

I believe I will take the time to tell you that there will come a time when somebody comes to church and all they want to hear is Jesus. I don't know if there are any preachers in this house but let me tell you something.

When folk crawl in between these rows and they have nothing to hold on to but the word you preach, preach Jesus.

When you stand by a lonely bedside in a hospital room and the hand you hold is of a woman being eaten away with cancer, don't read from a book. I can read from the book myself. What I need is somebody that can get in touch with Jesus. I need somebody who can call on Jesus and get an answer. I need somebody who will put formality aside and preach Jesus.

When you go to the home of a member and there you find a battered wife and abused children, that's no time to be holier-than-thou, that's the time to tell that wife there is hope for tomorrow; that's the time to tell somebody with tears in their eyes that there is a bright side somewhere; that's the time to tell that child that they are still a child of God; that's the time to pick up this Word and preach Jesus.

When the homeless make their way to church on Sunday morning you need to remember that the only reason you are not homeless, the only reason you're not down and out, the only reason you have shoes on both your feet and gas in your car is because of God's amazing grace. So here's what you do: put your arm around someone you don't know, put your arm around someone who doesn't look like you look, someone who does not dress like you dress, and smell as you smell, and preach Jesus.

And yet, it is not enough to tell someone who follows in my wake to "Preach Jesus." Authentic preaching has an antecedent. God-kissed preaching has a priority that comes before. There is, as the scholars speak of it, an a'priori factor. There is something else that must occur before preaching takes place. It has a higher priority. And this is what it is: **Anointment comes before Appointment.** Before you stand to preach Jesus it is required that there is an anointment on your life.

Anointment—'tis old fashioned to speak of such things in sophisticated company.

Anointment—what meaningless, archaic and barbaric religious ritual is this?

Anointment—who in this day and age has time for the pouring and smearing of oil?

Forgive my archaic language, humor me if you will, but the reason too many churches are falling apart, the reason too many preachers are mounting pulpits without power, the reason, I tell you, that too many Sunday mornings nothing happens in the pulpit or the pew is because there is no anointment.

Even Jesus had to get in the anointing line. Luke remembered it and wrote it down:

> *"The Spirit of the Lord is upon me,*
> *Because He hath anointed me to*
> *preach the gospel to the poor;*
> *He hath sent me to heal the brokenhearted,*
> *To preach deliverance to the captives,*
> *And recovering of sight to the blind,*
> *To set at liberty them that are bruised,*
> *To preach the acceptable year of the Lord."*

Don't tell me you are called to preach until you have first been called to the fountain of anointment. Talk to me about your anointment...

- An anointment is a confirmation of the cosmic intention of God in your life.
- An anointment is a divine consecration that human hands can never defile.

- An anointment is an affidavit of heaven dictated by the mouth of God, entered into the record by Alpha and ushered into the archives of Eternity by Omega.

- An anointment is a blessing of benediction that only God can give and none can take away.

- An anointment is the fresh flowing power of the Holy Spirit that is operative in your life.

- An anointment is the equipping agent for those who would be involved in a ministry designed to turn the world upside down.

There is a reason for my anointment. It is only by the power of the anointing that I am able to preach Jesus. I am called to preach but my preaching is *covered* by the anointing. The only reason the anointing is a functional part of my spiritual life is because I am *covered* by the anointing of God that mere mortal men may not be able to see.

Dangers may be all around me but I am covered by the anointing.

I may walk through the valley and the shadow of death but I am covered by the anointing.

Sometime I came in here and my head was bowed beneath my knees but I was covered by the anointing.

Sometime weapons were formed against me but I am covered by the anointing. Let me tell you why:

The anointing is marked by the pouring of oil over the head and permitted to run down the head of the one upon whom God's hand has been laid. The anointment is marked by the pouring on of oil, set aside and sacred, that is symbolic of the Holy Spirit.

The name **CHRIST** means "the anointed one." So, when I am anointed, I am anointed as Christ is anointed. When I am anointed it is then that I am most like Christ, moving under the power of Christ, empowered by the instruction of Christ and preaching under the authority of Christ.

When I am anointed I am preaching not because I have usurped divinity but because I am empowered as anointed humanity. That means that in my human state there is nothing that I can do, but in my anointed state there is nothing that I cannot do. In fact, says Paul, **"I can do all things through Christ which strengtheneth me."**

When the oil is poured over the head it means that I am totally covered by the Holy Spirit. I am totally covered ... from my head to my feet. Let me tell you how:

> *The Lord is my Shepherd; I shall not want:*
> *He maketh me to lie down in green pastures:*
> *He leadeth me beside the still waters*
> *He restoreth my soul*

He leadeth me in the paths of righteousness
for His namesake
Yea though I walk through the valley and
the shadow of death

I will fear no evil
For thou art with me
Thou preparest a table before me in
the presence of my enemies
Thou anointest my head with oil
My cup runneth over.
Surely, goodness and mercy shall follow me
all the days of my life
And I shall dwell in the House of the Lord
forever.

This is what I've been trying to tell you:

For 37 years, I've been covered.

For 37 years, I've been in His hands. I've been covered.

For 37 years and more, all night, all day, angels have been watching over me. I've been covered.

I've been up sometime and down sometime, but for 37 years I've been covered.

Sometime in sickness, sometime in pain, but for 37 years I've been covered.

Sometimes I didn't feel like preaching, didn't want to get out of bed on Sunday morning, but I've been covered.

Sometimes I felt as though I was preaching another disastrous sermon in a disastrous situation but let me tell you, honey, I've got a covering over me.

Paul says it this way: *"I speak as a fool. I am more. In labors more abundant, in stripes above measure, in prisons more frequent, in deaths oft."* But I've been covered.

Paul says it this way: *"For I am not ashamed of the gospel of Christ for it is the power of God unto salvation to everyone that believeth, to the Jew first, and also to the Greek."* I've been covered.

What else, Paul? "We are troubled on every side, yet not distressed; we are perplexed but not in despair; persecuted but not forsaken, cast down but not destroyed." I've been covered. And so, I preached Jesus.

Read carefully Paul's word for what he writes here is critical. "For I determined (I made up my mind, I am satisfied in mind and spirit) not to know anything among you, save Jesus Christ and Him crucified." In other words, Paul's preaching is the preaching of the Cross.

Hear me today. You and I stand in the long train of the prophets whose words give light to the Word of God. But in the end, we must preach the Cross. I am enamored with Amos and Hosea and Ezekiel. But in the end, we must preach the Cross.

I have no quarrel with academic religionists. Yet I know that I am no systematic theologian. I am no biblical scholar; I am no archeologist sent to unearth hidden treasures of the Word. I have no gift to study ancient languages but I know this: In the end we must preach the Cross.

I might as well tell you, you have not preached until you make your way to the cross. I might as well tell you that much of our preaching is powerless because preachers are preaching but they see no value in the cross. Peaching is not preaching unless and until it has the blood of Golgotha's tree spilled upon it. Dr. Gardner Taylor suggests that no matter where the preacher starts in his preaching he must, as quickly as possible, make his way cross-country to Calvary.

Much of our worship is anemic because we sing our Praise Songs but those songs very often have no appreciation for the Cross, they see no value in the Cross. I don't know about you but I still like to sing:

> *Jesus keep me near the cross*
> *There a precious fountain,*
> *Free to all a healing stream*
> *Flows from Calvary's mountain.*

I don't know about you but I still like to sing:

> *Alas and did my Saviour bleed*
> *And did my Sovereign die?*
> *Would He devote that Sacred Head*
> *For such a worm as I?*

I don't know about you but I still like to sing:

> *Down at the Cross where my Savior died;*
> *Down where for cleansing from sin I cried.*
> *There to my heart was the blood applied,*
> *Singing glory to His name.*

I preach Jesus but I still preach the cross.

Listen, we began this homily with a discussion on disastrous preaching. And disastrous preaching, loosely defined, has to do with sermons where nothing happens. No changed lives, no converted souls, no shouts of praise or sounds of Hallelujah!

But I'm here today to tell you that:

- if we preach the Cross something will happen.
- If we preach Jesus crucified, dead, buried, resurrected, and coming again something will happen.
- If we preach the Cross someone will lift up Holy Hands.
- If we preach the Cross still hands will clap together.
- If we preach the Cross a cold pulpit will catch on fire and a frigid pew will find its seats aflame.
- If we preach the Cross the angels in heaven will bend low to hear the sound.
- If we preach the Cross mortal tongues will learn an immortal language.
- If we preach the Cross someone will accuse us of being drunk on new wine.
- If we preach the Cross the church will find a "demonstration of the spirit and of power."

If we preach the Cross sinners will be converted, lives will be redeemed and the redeemed of the Lord will "say so." And that's why ...

I **still** preach the Cross. "It was the third hour, and they crucified Him."

I still preach the Cross. "Unto us which are saved it is the power of God."

I still preach the Cross. "We preach Christ crucified, unto the Jews a stumbling block, and unto the Greeks foolishness."

I still preach the Cross: "Who for the joy that was set before Him endured the cross, despising the shame."

Hear me today, I will still preach Jesus and I still preach Calvary's Cross! I still preach a rugged cross. I still preach an "emblem of suffering and shame." I still preach a blood soaked cross. I still preach the cross.

Well, Brother Pastor, what have you done for all these years?

For 37 years
I preached Jesus.

I tried to help somebody as I passed along.
I preached Jesus.

I didn't want my living to be in vain so
I preached Jesus

I studied to show myself approved unto God, rightly dividing the word of truth.
I preached Jesus.

I decided to follow Jesus so
I preached Jesus.

The world behind me, the Cross before me
I preached Jesus.

Just as I am without one plea
I preached Jesus.

Jesus is all the world to me, my life, my joy, my all
I preached Jesus.

In season and out of season,
I preached Jesus.

My witness is in heaven and my record will be there.
I preached Jesus.

On Jordan's stormy banks I stand to cast a wishful eye
I preached Jesus.

To Canaan's fair and happy land where my possessions lie
I preached Jesus.

Though the storms keep on raging in my life,
My soul's been anchored in the Lord
I preached Jesus.

And ... when I feel the mist of ol' chilly Jordan spraying in my face,
> I will preach Jesus.

> *Sweet hour of prayer, sweet hour of prayer*
> *may I thy consolation share?*
> *Till from Mount Pisgah's lofty height,*
> *I view my home and take my flight.*

> *This robe of flesh I'll drop and rise*
> *to seize the everlasting prize.*
> *And shout while passing through the air,*
> *"Farewell, farewell sweet hour of prayer.*

Appendix

The Rev. Dr. William Barber, President, North Carolina NAACP, Speech Transcript, Democratic National Convention, July 28, 2016, printed by author's permission.

"Good evening, my Brothers and Sisters.

I come before you tonight as a preacher, the son of a preacher, a preacher immersed in the movement at five years old. *I don't come tonight representing any organization, but I come to talk about faith and morality.*

I'm a preacher and *I'm a theologically conservative liberal evangelical Biblicist.* I know it may sound strange, but I'm a conservative because I work to conserve a divine tradition that teaches us to do justice, love mercy, and walk humbly with our God.

I've had the privilege of traveling the country with the Reverend Dr. James Forbes, and Reverend Dr. Traci Blackmon and Sister Simone Campbell as we are working together in the revival and calling for a revolution of values.

And as we travel the country, we see things. *That is why I'm so concerned, about those that say so much—about what God says so little, while saying so little—about what God says so much. And so in my heart, I'm troubled.*

And I'm worried about the way faith is cynically used by some to serve hate, fear, racism and greed.

We need to heed the voice of the Scriptures. We need to listen to the ancient chorus in which "deep calls unto deep." The prophet Isaiah cries out, "What I'm interested in seeing you doing, says the Lord, as a nation is, 'Pay people what they deserve' 'Share your food with the hungry.' Do this and then your nation shall be called a repairer of the breach."

Jesus, a brown skinned Palestinian Jew, *called us to preach good news to the poor, the broken, and the bruised, and all those who are made to feel dispossessed.*

Our constitution calls us to commit our government to establish justice, to promote the general welfare, to provide for the common defense and to ensure domestic tranquility.

Now, to be true, we've never lived this vision perfectly. But this ought to be the goal at the heart of our democracy. *And when religion is used to camouflage meanness, we know that we have a heart problem in America.*

There have always been forces that want to harden and even stop the heart of democracy. There have also always been people who stood together to a stir what sister Dorothy called "the revolution of the heart" and what Dr. King called a "radical revolution of values."

I say to you tonight, *there are some issues that are not Left versus Right, Liberal versus Conservative, they are* "right versus wrong."

We need to embrace our deepest moral values and push for a revival of the heart of our democracy.

- When we fight to *reinstate the power of the Voting Rights Act* and to break interposition and the nullification of the current Congress, we in the South especially know that when we do that, we are reviving the heart of our democracy.

- When we fight for *a union, and universal healthcare, and public education, and immigrant rights, and LGBTQ rights,* we are reviving the heart of our democracy.

- When we *develop tax and trade policies that no longer funnel our prosperity to the wealthy few,* we are reviving the heart of our democracy. We know we are reviving the heart of our democracy.

- When we hear the legitimate *discontent of Black Lives Matter and we come together to renew justice in our criminal justice system, we are embracing our deepest moral values* and reviving the heart of our democracy.

- When we *love the Jewish child and the Palestinian child, the Muslim and the Christian, and the Hindu, and the Buddhist, and those who have no faith— but they love this nation, we are reviving the heart of our democracy.*

- ⇝ When we fight for *peace and when we resist the proliferation of military style weapons on our streets, and when we stand against the anti-democratic stronghold of the NRA*, we are reviving the heart of our democracy.

In times like these, we have to make some decisions and I might not normally as a preacher, an individual, but when *I hear Hillary's voice and her positions, I hear and I know that she is working to embrace our deepest moral values — and we should embrace her.*

But let me be clear, let me be clear, that *she, nor any person, can do it alone. The watchword of this democracy and the watchword of faith is "WE."* The heart of our democracy is on the line this November and beyond.

No, my friends, they tell me that when the heart is in danger, somebody has to call an emergency code. And somebody with a good heart will bring a defibrillator to work on the bad heart. Because it is possible to shock a bad heart and revive the pulse. *In the season, when someone tries to harden and stop the heart of our democracy, we are being called like our foremothers and forefathers to be the moral defibrillator of our time.*

We must shock this nation with the power of love. We must shock this nation with the power of mercy. We must shock this nation and fight for justice for all. We can't give up on the heart of our democracy, not now, not ever!

And so, and so I stop by here tonight to ask,

- Is there a heart in this house?

- Is there a heart in America?

- Is there somebody that has a heart for the poor, and a heart for the vulnerable?

- Then Stand up. Vote together. Organize together. *Fight for the heart of this nation.*

- And while you're are fighting, sing that old hymn: "Revive us again. Fill each heart with Thy love. May each soul be rekindled with fire from above. Hallelujah! Thine the glory. Hallelujah thine the glory. Revive us again."

Bibliography

Alcantara, Jared E., *Crossover Preaching*, Intervarsity Press, Downers Grove, Illinois, 2015.

Barth, Karl, (n.d.), AZQuotes. com. Retrieved August 25, 2017 from AZQuotes.com Web site http://www. azquotes.com/quote 689724.

Blount, Brian K. (ed.), *True to our Native Land*, Augsburg Press, Minneapolis, Minnesota, 2007.

Callahan, Allen, Unpublished Ordination Manuscript, Harvard University, first delivered at Metropolitan Baptist Church, Washington, D. C., 1997.

Cannon, Katie G., and Pinn, Anthony B., (eds.), *The Oxford Handbook of African American Theology*, Oxford University Press, Oxford, England, 2014.

Carter, Stephen L., *The Culture of Disbelief*, BasicBooks, HarperCollins, 1993
Cleveland, Ohio 2006.

Dyson, Michael, *The Black Presidency*. Houghton Mifflin Harcourt, New York, New York, 2016.

Johnson, James Weldon, *God's Trombones: Seven Negro Sermons in Verse*, Viking Press, New York, 1927.

Jones, William Augustus, *Responsible Preaching*, Aaron Press, 1989.

Keller, Timothy, *Preaching*, Viking Random House, New York, New York, 2015.

Kelly, Leontine T. C., *Preaching in the Black Tradition, Women Ministers*, Judith L. Weidman, (ed.), Harper and Row, Publishers, 1981.

Kenyatta, Gilbert R., *A Pursued Justice*, Baylor University Press, Baylor University, Baylor, Texas, 2016.

King, Martin Luther, *Stride toward Freedom*, Harper & Brothers, New York, New York, 1958.

Massey, James Earl, *The Preacher's Rhetoric in A Celebration of Ministry*: Essays in Honor of Frank Bateman Stanger, Francis Asbury Publishing Company, Inc.

McKenzie, Vashti M., *Not Without a Struggle*, The Pilgrim Press, Cleveland, Ohio, 1996.

McMickle, Marvin A., *Pulpit and Politics*, Judson Press, Valley Forge, Pennsylvania, 2014.

McMickle, Marvin, *Where Have All the Prophets Gone?* The Pilgrim Press, Cleveland, Ohio, 2006.

National Baptist Hymn Book, worded edition, *Go Preach My Gospel* (meter hymn) National Baptist Publishing Board, Nashville, Tennessee, 1906.

Sanders, Cheryl J. , *African American Religious Studies: An Interdisciplinary Anthology, The Woman as Preacher,* Gayraud Wilmore (ed.), Duke University Press, Durham and London, 1989.

Simmons, Martha and Thomas, Frank A., *Preaching with Sacred Fire,* W. W. Norton and Company, New York, 2010.

Taylor, Gardner, *How Shall They Preach?* Lyman Beecher Lectures. Progressive Baptist Publishing House, Elgin, Illinois, 1977.

The Holy Bible, Authorized King James Version, Zondervan Press, Grand Rapids, Michigan, 2009.

Thomas, Gerald Lamont, (ed), *African-American Preaching*, Peter Lang Publishing, Inc.

Thomas, Gerald Lamont, *African American Preaching*: The Contribution of Dr. Gardner C. Taylor, Peter Lang Publishing, Inc., New York, p.109

Webster's New World Dictionary, Second College edition 1986.

Weems, Renita J. *Listening for God: A Minister's Journey through Silence and Doubt*, Touchstone/Simon Schuster, New York, NY.

Weidman, Judith L. (ed.), *Women Ministers*, Harper and Row, Publishers, San Francisco, 1981.

Weidman, Judith L., *The Woman as Preacher in Women Ministers*, Harper and Row, San Francisco, 1971.

. . .

About the Author

A native of Baton Rouge, Louisiana, H. Beecher Hicks, Jr. is the progeny of a family of educators, preachers, preaching and the Lord's Church. Licensed and ordained by the Mount Olivet Church of Columbus, Ohio, Dr. Hicks diligently honed his skills in homiletics at Colgate Rochester Divinity School, Rochester, NY (D. Min.) and his leadership and business skills at the George Washington University School of Business in the District of Columbia. (MBA) Hicks' ministry has spanned over fifty years and includes the pastorate of four congregations—Mumford, New York, Pittsburgh, Pennsylvania, Houston, Texas, and for thirty-seven years, Metropolitan Baptist Church in Washington D. C.

As to work in the academy, Dr. Hicks has served as Adjunct Professor of homiletics at several notable schools, including Howard University School of Divinity, United Theological Seminary, University of Chicago, and Colgate Rochester Divinity School. In the year 2015 the Wesley Theological Seminary designated Dr. Hicks as Distinguished Visiting Professor of Homiletics.

As to preaching, his voice has been heard in storefronts, chapels, college campuses, churches and Cathedrals across the globe. In the year 2000, the Baptist World Alliance selected this preacher to deliver the keynote address for its conference in Melbourne, Australia, an audience from nations around the globe. In 2010 the E. K Bailey Expository Preaching Conference honored Dr. Hicks as a *Living Legend* among preachers of this generation. Selected by his peers, Dr. Hicks was honored as *Conference Preacher* for the Hampton University Ministers' Conference, an annual conference of over ten thousand delegates. Annually, Dr. Hicks has been invited to preach for the Services at Rankin Chapel, Howard Divinity School. Most recently Dr. Hicks has been invested with the honorary doctor of Humane Letters from Morehouse College of Atlanta, Georgia.

Among his writings, *Images of the Black Preacher* (Dissertation: Judson Press 1977) and *Preaching Through a Storm* (Zondervan 1985) are classic representations of his ministry in print. He is married to the former Elizabeth Harrison (Selma, Alabama 1965) and together they are the parents of H. Beecher, III., Ivan Douglas Hicks (Indianapolis, Ind.), and Kristin Elizabeth (Mitchellville, Md.). For more information, please visit hbeecherhicksministries.com.

. . .

Reading Group Guide

The following questions are suggested conversation starters for groups interested in fleshing out the substance of this work. Groups are encouraged to contact Dr. Hicks to arrange for him to join your discussion via conference call. To do so, please contact Dr. Hicks' personal assistant, Minister E. Missy Daniels, at mdanwalls@aol. com.

Chapter 1
- Does preaching matter? Why do you think it remains relevant and needed today?
- Why must the Kerygma be proclaimed?
- What is your task as a preacher?

Chapter 2
- To whom do you owe the debt of preaching?
- What are the lessons for preaching?
  » *Read the recipe (Bible), have the ingredients lined neatly in a row has no value (be creative)*
  » *A private word intended for the Preacher/Baker (persistence and fortitude are essential, there is no such thing as "perfection.")*

- » *Don't leave anything out (preach the whole Bible)*
- » *Don't forget the icing.*
- Name the seven pillars. Why are they essential?
- What is the pillar you need most to work on?

Chapter 3

- Name two things that silence the prophetic voice in the Church?
- What do you think the preacher needs to provide? How do you as a preacher adjust to address those needs?
- Are social issues critical to the prophetic voice? What are the issues prevalent in your church community and surrounding neighborhoods?
- What are doctrinal watchwords? What, in your estimation, are the new watchwords?
- Do you think God calls us to give both to a prophetic culture, prophetic pedagogy and/or prophetic mission? Why?
- Where are the places to preach prophetically?
- Why is prevenient causality important to the prophet?

Chapter 4

- As you find your own voice, what does it sound like? Who has influenced you? Mentored you? What do you want to improve upon?
- True/False: You are in search of an anointment that empowers you to seek and accomplish what is in you — authentic and real. What is your reality?
- What is your anointment? How is it connected to your assignment?

Chapter 5

- What forces and sources have impacted communities to which you have been called to minister
- What factors make the prophet bleed? Why? Which influences you the most?
- Why has it become difficult to fulfill our task in preaching?
- What factors make our religion authentic?
- In what ways do we bleed? Do we bleed alone?

Chapter 6

- What is authentic preaching? How should it impact the preacher?
- What two things is the preacher obligated to do? List them.

- When writing your sermon what are you waiting on? Why?
- There are many methods of preaching, which one is the best? Why?
- "The sermon should be a wedding between creative homiletics and hermeneutical accuracy." Explain this statement's significance.

Chapter 7

- As an expression of faith — what is religion intended to be?
- As humanity asks the question of incredulity to God, what question does God ask humanity?
- What are the two ways God knows you're serious?
- Faith without sacrifice is pointless. Sacrifice without faith is dangerous. Why?

www.ingramcontent.com/pod-product-compliance
Lightning Source LLC
Chambersburg PA
CBHW032125160426
43197CB00008B/518